PERSPECTIVES ON THE NEWS

REINVENTING *the* NEWSPAPER

Essays by

Frank Denton   Howard Kurtz

Series Editor: Suzanne Charlé

A Twentieth Century Fund Paper

The Twentieth Century Fund is a research foundation undertaking timely analyses of economic, political, and social issues. Not-for-profit and nonpartisan, the Fund was founded in 1919 and endowed by Edward A. Filene.

Library of Congress Cataloging-in-Publication Data

Denton, Frank, 1945–
    Reinventing the newspaper : essays / by Frank Denton and Howard Kurtz.
    p. cm. -- (Perspectives on the news : 3)
    Includes index.
    ISBN 0-87078-350-5 : $9.95
    1. American newspapers--History--20th century. I. Kurtz, Howard, 1953– . II. Title. III. Series.
PN4867.D43 1993
071'.30904--dc20

93-9255
CIP

Cover Design and Illustration: Claude Goodwin
Manufactured in the United States of America.

Foreword

A t the advent of the twentieth century, a normal city morning began with the clatter of horses' hooves on the cobblestones. A decade or two later, when the honking of horns provided an added wake-up call, it still was possible to believe that the automobile would be a supplement, not a substitute for the horse. Now, near the dawn of another century, the sound of the morning newspaper being delivered is increasingly drowned out by the voices of the "Today" show, headline news, and NPR.

Technology has changed society in many ways; few of those changes are more pervasive and less understood than the electronic media that have engulfed our daily lives. Broadcasting has altered more than journalism and the economics of newspapers. Television and radio affect the way all of us are governed, entertained, and hustled—in other words, the way we experience the world. The rise of these media and their success in attracting audiences and advertisers also has put enormous financial pressure on print publications. True, many newspapers still prosper, apparently in coexistence with the new media, often even setting the news agenda for "shows" that report over the air. But the newspapers as we know them may well be on the way to joining the buggy whip and the milk wagon in some museum of the American past. Nostalgia aside, if so, does it matter?

The American system of journalism has grown up with the notion that the marketplace, especially through advertising revenues, frees newspapers from dependence upon and the control of government or party. However uneven in effect, this consequence of free enterprise is no trivial virtue. But dependence on the marketplace means that the business of journalism is subject to the same forces of "creative destruction" that bring general economic change. Although such upheavals are commendable, theoretically, in terms of economic efficiency, they often trample other values.

What is at stake here is the traditional role of the newspaper as representative and even champion of a wide range of community values. While large metropolitan newspapers publish different editions for different areas within their regions, the bulk of their coverage is still community-wide. Newspapers thus help to create a common frame of reference for citizens, and they do so with a depth of coverage and analysis that is seldom matched by their electronic cousins. But today all media face fragmentation of their audiences, a phenomenon that is likely to increase as hundreds of cable television channels become the norm. In response, potential innovations in newspaper delivery systems may allow greater individualism. While these and other technological advances may permit newspapers to survive the trend toward smaller and more specialized media audiences, they also may speed the dissolution of whatever degree of community remains.

The essays that follow are part of the Twentieth Century Fund's continuing series, Perspectives on the News. In them, Frank Denton, editor of the *Wisconsin State Journal* and formerly an editor at the *Detroit Free Press*, and Howard Kurtz, the *Washington Post*'s media reporter and author of *Media Circus: The Trouble with America's Newspapers*, explore some of the difficult questions about the future of newspapers in America, and carefully examine the opportunities for and limits of future adaptations by newspapers to the changing landscape of American media. Both brought great experience and fresh insight to the task. On behalf of the Fund's Trustees, I thank them for their contributions to this timely and significant subject.

Richard C. Leone, *President*
The Twentieth Century Fund
April 1993

Contents

Old Newspapers and New Realities: The Promise of the Marketing of Journalism

by Frank Denton

Who Reads the Newspaper?

A t 6:45 A.M., still in the dark, the newspaper reader slips on her bathrobe, tugs on her galoshes, trudges through the snow out to the curbside tube, and extracts her morning newspaper. Reversing her steps, she completes the process, pours a cup of coffee and—after flicking on the television to "Good Morning America"—finally settles down to read the paper.

In her daily ritual, she grips the paper at the corner of the fold, holds it out and shakes it, freeing a cascade of advertising inserts. Setting those aside for possible reference later, she quickly checks the front-page headlines for any earthshaking news. No, just the predictable: violence in the Balkans, intransigence in the Middle East, rhetoric in Washington, and more worrisome crime in town. She reorganizes the sections according to her personal preferences: national and foreign news, and local news, then sports, leaving the features section—with its comics—as a final reward.

While an attractive television anchor smiles through a live report of food lines and violence in Eastern Europe, the reader finishes the first section and picks up the metro section. She scans the first page for something interesting or important to read:

"The city council Tuesday agreed to consider extending the urban service boundaries. . . ."

"This year's United Way campaign raised a record $16 million, surpassing its goal. . . ."

"One woman died and her two children were hospitalized Tuesday after a three-car collision. . . ."

"The city planning commission agreed Tuesday night to rezone a parcel of land from industrial to commercial to allow development. . . ."

Nothing there for her; if she is going to think, it will be about her new car loan or her weekend plans or the tough day's work ahead. Her

3

eye catches on a story about the House bank scandal, causing her to shake her head at the whole Washington bunch—politicians of every stripe and bureaucrats and, yes, their media cronies. In disgust, she skips on. With diminishing patience, the clock's hands moving, she quickly pages through the sections—perhaps only out of routine, but also semiconsciously in search of something to pull her in. Whenever she comes across something within her range of possible interest, the stories just don't get her involved: With the television's audio and visual teasing, or nagging, somehow the newspaper's writing or words or presentation just doesn't connect. She is not, however, fully aware of the dynamics of this little morning ritual.

By now, the anchor has introduced a celebrity interview, and the reader looks up and becomes a viewer. Hooked, she sets the paper aside and watches until she notices it is 7:15 and time to get ready for work. She stands up, rolls her eyes at the ink ruboff on her bathrobe, tosses the paper, mostly unread, into the recycling pile and turns up the television volume so she can listen while she dresses.

That scene, repeated in millions of American homes every day, illustrates a set of phenomena contributing to the accelerating erosion of the presence and power of the daily newspaper:

▲ While electronic media are omnipresent throughout the home, the newspaper still is delivered as it was fifty years ago, oftentimes no nearer than the street, perhaps dry and perhaps not. The television set, with its instant-on feature, is always warm and ready to entertain.

▲ While television is as immediate as it wants to be, the newspaper is at least five hours old, usually older.

▲ The newspaper has ink ruboff, mediocre color reproduction, and still photographs, mostly black and white. Television has audio and video and full color and graphics.

▲ Newspaper advertising inserts clutter the house. Television allows zapping and, when taped, zipping.

▲ The newspaper costs as much as $200 a year and by law in many places must be recycled, in neat bundles no more than six inches thick, firmly tied with twine and carried to the curb on the correct day of the week. Television is free—some of it at least—and appears and disappears with a click.

And finally, even with all that, the toughest barriers to newspaper readership may be the most intimate:

▲ Television is entertainment. Even news programs are called shows, the viewers are called audiences, the anchors are chosen for their attractiveness and the news for its visual potential. Television news reaches the viewer at the affective—feeling—level, while the very nature of the newspaper demands cognition, thinking.

▲ Viewing or listening can occur across a wide range of personal involvement, with the viewer/listener passive or active, committed or uncommitted. Reading, on the other hand, is intense, consuming, and intellectual—actually work for some people.

▲ Time, to many people, has become as valuable as money, because there seems to be less of it. People can do other things in front of the television set; reading demands complete attention.

▲ Through the citizenry's growing sense of noncredibility and alienation, combined with all the above, the newspaper no is longer the comfortable, essential routine it once was.

Americans have diminished their reliance on the daily newspaper and found they can live quite nicely, thank you, without it. In fact, an increasingly cynical and distrustful nation has developed an active dislike of news media generally, lumping them among the institutions responsible for the country's problems.

As all these factors have converged over the past decade or two—accelerating and intensifying in interactions with technology, the economy, and Americans' lives — daily newspaper circulation and readership have flattened, and market penetration, as a percentage of households, has declined with depressing regularity, plunging from a peak of more than 1.3 newspapers per home per day just after World War II to less than 0.7 paper in 1990.

The fall has been so steady that newspaper editors and executives have been able merely to worry about it, with appropriate concern discussed at industry meetings then mostly forgotten at home. Publishers' and editors' bookshelves are filled with ominous reports, which they were able to disregard throughout the 1980s because the money always was there.

As Howard Kurtz points out in his companion paper, newspapers have been among the most profitable of businesses in this century. As, at least, oligopolies and, increasingly, monopolies, newspapers generally have had their way with advertisers, who provide 75 to 85 percent of a newspaper's revenue. Radio and television may have been best at image advertising and at mass-communicating a simple advertising headline—"The new Saturns finally are in," "Filbert's annual sale starts Monday." But the major advertisers who needed to communicate information, such as multiple products and prices—notably department and grocery stores—required those expensive full-page ads. Especially with the coming of cable television, it simply was easier for an advertiser to buy one newspaper broadly circulated to an affluent audience than to try to pull together several television stations and the cable system for comparable breadth of reach. Add the small retail advertisers, who couldn't afford electronic media, and classified advertisers, who required the special characteristics and economy of the newspaper, and the publisher's main problems were keeping an eye on costs and counting the money. Pushed by the perennial growth demands of the stock market, profit margins grew and grew, commonly beyond 20 and even 30 percent—compared to the low single digits for the ordinary retailers who bought the ads.

Suddenly, within the past half-dozen years and intensifying in the 1990–92 recession, everything is changing. Newspaper executives were slapped with new numbers they no longer could explain away or ignore. Newspaper advertising revenue declined in 1990 for the first time since 1970, and only the second time since 1961. Then in 1991, it fell another 5 percent, the worst percentage decline since 1942, according to one analyst.[1]

While the free-fall of advertising was not caused primarily by the declining readership, the two together have brought the daily newspaper into a cataclysm that is profoundly changing this venerable, if not venerated, American institution. Just as newspaper journalism seemed to be approaching a reasonable level of professionalism and sophistication, and newspapers became better than ever, the sources of their strength have begun to wither.

To many people today, the newspaper seems an anachronism, a once-powerful, hyperprofitable institution suddenly come upon hard times, its wealthy owners and comfortable executives confused, stammering, looking around and wondering what happened, what to do. In an era of efficiency, streamlining, firestorm innovation, and breathtaking technology, newspapers smell of the industrial past: big buildings, dinosaur presses, labor intensity, oil-based ink on landfill-clogging paper . . . hand delivery!

One question that must be asked is, Who—aside from people with a financial interest—cares? Why worry about saving what many see as an obnoxious, negative, parasitic business? Who truly likes newspapers anyway?

The easy answer is that few people care, and many even are enjoying watching the arrogant, greedy newspaper getting its due.

The thoughtful answer is that, for the sake of our democracy, we must care. For all their faults, newspapers perform social and political functions—as monitor, watchdog, forum, catalyst—that, for now at least, cannot be replaced by a tube.

The issue is what must be done. In a time of tumult and peril, newspapers may be focusing on the issue myopically, on what is wrong with them, rather than what has changed with Americans and their relationship with newspapers. Perhaps they must change together.

Ironically, salvation, or at least survival, may lie in a discipline that journalists long have distrusted and disparaged: marketing. Aside from all the potential friction between prosocial journalism and the profit demands of the marketplace, marketing in its purest form is providing ideas, goods, and services in exchanges that satisfy the consumer and the provider. It is finding, or creating, a need and filling it, and in this society, this democracy, there is great need for responsive, thoughtful, aggressive, quality newspaper journalism.

If the daily newspaper were just another consumer product, it would not be seen as venerable, just old. Marketing analysts chart a product life cycle in four major stages: introduction, growth, maturity, and decline. Newspapers are in the maturity phase facing decline, with flat industry sales and even declining profits. That stage traditionally calls for defensive, passive strategies, perhaps leading to a temptation to accept the inevitability of death and move into harvesting—cutting production and marketing costs, minimally maintaining existing products and customers, and extracting what profits remain in the market.

If the newspaper were just another consumer product, it would be assessed that dispassionately, that coldly. A marketer would evaluate the effectiveness of the newspaper by analyzing and understanding its relationship with its customers methodically, at various levels and degrees of complexity. One framework, among many that might offer insights, would apply the hard standards of marketing communication, that is, advertising effectiveness. From the perspective of the market, rather than the product, this framework would examine consumers' motivation, opportunity, and ability to accept and comprehend the communication. The framework is referred to as MOA.[2] If the newspaper were evaluated as rigorously as advertising is, one could ask whether the American public still has the same motivation, opportunity, and ability to process its messages.

Motivation: Why Should One Bother?

When consumer-behavior researchers examine individuals' response to advertising or other exposure to products, they commonly first consider "involvement"—the level of one's perceived interest in the message or the product. In other words, what's in it for the consumer?

When asked in surveys why they read the newspaper, that is, the nature and depth of their involvement, readers tend to cite the most socially acceptable reasons. The Newspaper Readership Project, sponsored by the Newspaper Advertising Bureau during 1977 to 1983, found that 72 percent of those surveyed said the "single most important reason" they read the paper was to keep up with current events and stay informed. Advertising, at 26 percent, came in second, and after that, readers named specific parts of the paper, such as sports, business, or local news; 22 percent mentioned habit or the social or psychological gratifications of reading.[3]

Two things may be undercutting the primary motivation of staying informed about current events.

First, the simple, seductive alternative—what consumer-behavior analysts call product substitution. When time contracts and pressures build, readers who want to feel informed can find it easy to click on the television and get the news in an entertaining, nondemanding way. For twenty-five years, Americans have been telling surveyors that television is their main source of news about current affairs (an unfounded belief, as we shall see later).

Second, the desire to stay informed also may be lost in people who are alienated from, or simply uninterested in, public affairs, the core content of a typical daily newspaper. "Public ignorance and apathy seem to be the enduring legacy of twenty-five hundred years of political evolution," W. Russell Neuman writes in *The Paradox of Mass Politics*.[4] Neuman notes that only during times of national crisis—such as war, depression, or a Watergate-type scandal—do a majority of Americans pay much attention to government and politics. An average one-third of the voting-age population admit they do not even care who is elected president, a proportion that has increased in recent years, peaking at half in 1976. Low voter turnout (averaging 59 percent in presidential years, at least until the unusual 1992 campaign; 42 percent in other years) is nothing new, and Neuman states that only 12 percent of adults have ever signed a petition, 5 percent have contributed to a political candidate, 4 percent have written a government official, and only 2 percent have participated in a political demonstration. "Over the past two decades," Neuman writes, "... on average, 56 percent of the population have been unable to identify any congressional candidate in their district at the height of the congressional campaign." A January 1993 survey by the Times Mirror

Center for the People and the Press found that—while 40 percent of Americans watched at least one of the made-for-TV movies about Amy Fisher—only 21 percent could name any Clinton appointee, 23 percent said they were keeping up with the civil war in Bosnia.

In contrast, Americans seem far more willing to become involved in public affairs at the local level, in their neighborhoods and in their schools. Through focus groups in ten cities in 1991, researchers for the Kettering Foundation concluded that the difference is the degree to which people feel involved and empowered to have an effect. Many citizens who would be involved in national and state affairs have withdrawn because they think that they don't make a difference. More specifically, Americans feel that the issues that dominate politics are not their true concerns, that the discussion of issues does not connect with real people, and that even the language used by politicians and professionals is incomprehensible. They believe that special interests, political action committees, and lobbyists really control everything, that public officials no longer are responsive to ordinary people. "They feel politically impotent," the report concluded.[5]

It should be alarming to newspaper people that—contrary to their self-image as independent, iconoclastic watchdogs—the Kettering study found that people tend to see journalists and big media as part of the game that has taken control of public affairs. That should be no surprise: A 1985 American Society of Newspaper Editors survey on credibility reported that 36 percent of respondents believed the news media often are manipulated by powerful people.[6]

The supreme game, of course, is Washington, the federal establishment, politicians, bureaucrats, and their fraternity brothers, the Washington press corps. As one small example, consider the famous Nixon memo of early 1992, when the former president argued that the dissolution of the Soviet Union was far more important than was being recognized, that the Bush administration's response was dangerously inadequate, and that the United States hurriedly should lead a massive effort to shore up Russian democracy. It was an important analysis, particularly coming from the perspective of Richard Nixon. One would think he could disseminate his thinking merely by issuing it, but that is not how things are done in D.C. In a fascinating paper,[7] Marvin Kalb, himself a Washington media veteran who now directs a center for the study of the press and politics at Harvard, traced Nixon's clever and careful placement of a "private" memo designed to create maximum exposure and pressure Bush into action. The keys, of course, were well-placed journalists at the *New York Times, Washington Post,* and other media powers, insiders whose copies of the memo included a personal note from "RN." "Nixon knows the memo will leak, but he doesn't know how it will leak," Kalb wrote. "It's different each time. . . . Nixon not only understands the power of the print and electronic press, but he enjoys the manipulation of the press as a way of advancing his own agenda. He is fully familiar with the inter-relationship of press, politics, and public policy." As it turned out, *Time* magazine reported the memo on March 9, the *Post* and *Times* on March 10, the day before Nixon spoke on the subject at a Nixon Library conference in Washington.

What might an ordinary citizen, watching from Wisconsin, conclude from this little drama? That the media collaborate with one another and with those they cover? Or that powerful people like Nixon so easily can manipulate journalists eager to be part of the game? The specific interpretation may not matter. The citizen may just shake her head at the game itself, and tune out.

It does not require great imagination to see these phenomena interacting, that is, apathy and noncredibility feeding each other into a general ennui about public affairs and lack of interest in reading about them in the newspaper.

Without that primal involvement in the newspaper—keeping up with the news, the duty and self-interest of the citizen in a democratic society—what is left for the newspaper reader? A cafeteria of attributes, as editors like to say. Once, readers used the newspaper as entertainment, a pastime, or escape, but research shows that is less important today, perhaps eroded by the advent of readily available electronic entertainment, as well as by the likes of *People* magazine. Today, readers are more likely to look for specific content that satisfies their interests as shoppers, sports fans, puzzle-workers, help-seekers, editorial-debaters, consumers of the myriad pieces of the newspaper—television schedules, comics, bridge column, obituaries, financial listings, calendars.[8] Increasingly, such specific information and features are cheaper or more readily available elsewhere—talk radio, for example, and 900 phone services—and each new service cuts another of the complex, fragile ties between readers and the newspaper.

Opportunity: We Just Don't Have Time Anymore

The decline of what once was an American household fixture is occurring in a home where the occupants hardly have time to notice. For years, when newspaper circulators asked lapsed readers why they didn't renew their subscriptions, the common answer was time. As early as 1979, a major study found that 57 percent of dropouts from newspaper reading said they had less time than they once did.[9] In 1987, readers who recently had let their subscriptions lapse were asked to select "important" reasons from a list of thirteen: 40 percent said they "had no time to read," 38 percent said "papers just kept piling up before they got read," and 20 percent said they "had better things to do with my time."[10]

Conventional newspaper wisdom translated "time" into a catchall euphemism for cost or television addiction or lack of interest in public affairs—something that was "their fault." In the past few years, as editors have become less defensive, there has been some concession that maybe the editorial content is not as compelling as it might be—"our fault." Frustrated newspaper editors and reporters found no solace in a 1987 study for the American Society of Newspaper Editors (ASNE) that revealed: "Former subscribers evaluated highly the news and feature content of the daily newspaper they no longer had home-delivered. About three in ten consistently described the quality of the paper's news and feature content as 'excellent'; six in ten described it as 'good.'" The report was titled "Love Us and Leave Us."

In fact, when former readers tell us they don't have time, they probably mean just that.

The American life-style has accelerated and intensified to the point where simply taking the time to sit quietly and read is considered a luxury. Contrary to predictions of a generation ago—Whatever will we do with all the new leisure time? we wondered—Americans are more time-constrained than ever.[11] Everyone is working more and playing less than fifteen years ago.[12] Much of the pressure has been caused by the advent of a majority of women entering the work force: They retain most of their household duties, others are taken up by their male partners, and everyone's free time is reduced.

In her book *The Overworked American*,[13] economist Juliet B. Schor estimates that, compared to a generation ago, the average American worker is now on the job the equivalent of an extra month a year. She attributes this not only to employer demands but also to worker demand for enough pay to buy more consumer goods and services.

Meanwhile, Schor says, the time required for household work has not changed. Employed people are doing the same amount of housework they did twenty years ago; while women are doing fewer chores at home, men are doing more. Even with the shift of responsibility, various studies show that women who work full-time still come home to twenty-five to forty-five hours per week of labor at home.

How can that be, given all the new laborsaving machines we work so hard to buy? "Standards have crept up for nearly everything housewives do—laundry, cooking, care of children, shopping, care of the sick, cleaning," Schor says. Only in this century, and particularly in this country, have we become so fastidious about keeping our homes and our bodies constantly clean. While average household size has declined, the size of the house that has to be maintained has increased—from 750 square feet in the famous Levittown development of the 1950s to twice that by 1963 and to 2,000 square feet by 1989.

Then there is the third major responsibility, the family. Schor argues that today's model of devoted parenthood, with substantial investments of time and attention, is relatively new. In previous centuries, she says, parents were not nearly so bonded to their children, partly because many of them were not expected to survive, but also because both parents, as well as the children, had to work long hours for their own survival. Even with the modern devotion to childrearing, time constraints may be compromising the commitment: One study cited by Schor found that between 1960 and 1986, the time parents made available for their children fell ten hours a week for whites and twelve for blacks.

With all of that, what's left for the individual? In the past twenty years, the Harris Poll found, free time has declined more than 35 percent, from twenty-six hours per week to fewer than seventeen. Much of that nonwork time goes to shopping, spending all those extra dollars earned working overtime. Pointing out that Americans spend three to four times as many hours shopping as Europeans do, Schor calls it our "national passion." In 1990, the average American owned or consumed more than twice as much as in 1948, as measured by the gross national product.

Competing for the few remaining evening and weekend hours are the wide variety of personal and family activities, including relaxation, socializing, sports, exercise, hobbies, volunteer activities—and media usage, including the entire array of new electronic distractions such as videocassette recorders, video games, and personal computers.

It is worth pointing out that some researchers disagree with Schor. John P. Robinson, a sociologist who has studied time use for thirty years, maintains that Americans have more free time nowadays. But, he says, stress—such as "overchoice," facing too many life-style decisions—causes us to feel as if we are time-pressured.[14]

Whichever analysis one accepts, there is agreement that the big gorilla sitting in the middle of Americans' leisure time is television.

Robinson says people don't realize it, but they spend about half their leisure time parked in front of the tube. A 1992 study by the advertising agency Young & Rubicam found the average American adult spends three hours and forty-eight minutes a day watching television compared to thirty-four minutes reading newspapers.[15]

People are juggling so many things that they have become polychronic—what some consumer-behavior researchers call doing more than one thing at a time.[16] The best example may be the combining of television-watching (or listening) with another activity—cooking, playing a game, working on a hobby, or even reading. As we shall see, this is one phenomenon contributing to the failure of television as a medium for journalism.

Overall, Americans' time pressure has built to the point that 38 percent of the people surveyed in one poll reported cutting back on sleep to make more time and 70 percent (of those earning over $30,000 a year) said they would give up a day's pay each week for the extra free time.[17]

In light of the pressure from work, demands of home and family, and the passive, entertaining, relaxing lure of the television screen—where is there room for quiet, thoughtful reading time? Is it a wonder that the daily newspaper is no longer a routine in many American homes?

Ability: The Newspaper as a Puzzle

"Newspaper literacy" sounds incongruous, redundant perhaps: If one cannot read, he cannot read a newspaper; if one can read, she can read such common text. In fact, literacy is a continuum, not a dichotomy. Contrary to the popular, and sometimes politically exploited, image, very few Americans are utterly illiterate. Almost all of us possess varying reading skills that are situational, limited primarily by ever-changing reading demands in different settings.

The most substantial study of everyday American literacy was conducted in 1985 by the National Assessment of Educational Progress (NAEP), charged by Congress with evaluating the performance of young Americans in various learning areas. The final report noted:

> Based on the standard of "literacy" of a hundred years
> ago, the ability to sign one's name, virtually all young
> adults are "literate." If the standard of the World War
> II era, some fifty years ago, is applied, almost 95 per-
> cent of young adults are estimated to meet or exceed

the performance of fourth-grade students. Based on the standard of the War on Poverty, twenty-five years ago, 80 percent of young adults meet or exceed the performance of students in the eighth grade.[18]

Today, however, as society and technology become increasingly complex, ordinary Americans require far greater literacy skills just to get by—for example, to read appliance instructions, nutrition labeling, paycheck stubs, computer manuals, and, yes, information about complicated public issues.

In its national study of twenty-one- to twenty-five-year-olds, NAEP used a wide variety of tasks to simulate the diversity of literacy-related activities that people encounter in their daily lives. While the overwhelming majority were able to perform lower-level tasks, many fewer people were able to operate at the level of moderate complexity, and only a few could handle the most complex tasks. The falloff was particularly acute among minorities, especially blacks, and those with limited education. Examples, using two newspaper items: While 96 percent could retrieve a simple fact from a six-paragraph news story, only about 21 percent (approximately 25 percent of whites, 3 percent of blacks, 12 percent of Hispanics) could synthesize the main argument from a Tom Wicker column, a routine op-ed offering. The sharpest falloff was between locating information in a news article (56 percent: 63 percent of whites, 24 percent of blacks) and orally interpreting a lengthy feature story (37 percent: 43 percent of whites, 11 percent of blacks).

Yes, any of these young people can read the flavor of soup on the label, the NAEP found, but few of them can figure its unit price or comprehend its nutrition information. And, comics aside, the important parts of newspapers are beyond most of them. "The findings . . . clearly indicate that 'illiteracy' is not a *major* problem for the population of twenty-one- to twenty-five-year-olds," the report said. "It is also clear, however, that 'literacy' *is* a major problem" [emphasis in original].

Aliteracy is unwillingness to read on the part of a person who can read. Part of willingness derives from the reader—ability and motivation—but on the other side of the reading equation, to be considered interactively, are the demands, the difficulty of the text. Journalists are beginning to listen to critics who say that much of newspaper writing is artificial, contrived, confusing, and pedestrian. Ours is a tradition-bound discipline, and generations of young reporters have been taught reporting and writing skills that were developed during the early years of the newspaper, when the telegraph and the Linotype machine were the dominant technology.

The classic example is the inverted-pyramid story structure, which requires that the most important point of the story be in the first paragraph and that successive paragraphs or blocks of paragraphs be arranged in order of descending importance. That structure allowed readers, in the days before electronic media, to get the news flash first, and probably more important, it allowed editors bound by the constraints of deadlines and hot-lead typesetting to make stories fit on the page simply by tossing out entire sentences or paragraphs from the bottom. Another explanation of the tradition says that Civil War correspondents developed the inverted pyramid to guarantee they would be able to telegraph the most important parts of their stories before the wires went down. Although those reasons disappeared with the advent of reliable communication and computerized typesetting, the inverted pyramid continues to dominate American newspaper writing, and thus the reporting that precedes it.

In a 1979 paper for the Center for the Study of Reading at the University of Illinois at Urbana-Champaign,[19] Georgia M. Green dissected a routine Associated Press (AP) story about a Chicago protest against the shah of Iran. She found it "to some extent disorganized and undirected, unconnected and jumbled up, with the result that it is difficult to follow," even after she had rewritten the journalese out. Specifically, Green said the paragraphing did not organize the material, facts were not presented in a way helpful to readers, there were too many irrelevant details and too few connectives to show the relevance of facts to each other.

Green rewrote the story in three ways, as a sociologist proposing to study political protests, as one of the protesters might have told it, and as a reporter would describe it over dinner at home. She noted that, in pursuing the individual communication goals of each, the stories tended to organize themselves in comprehensible narrative styles, far different from the AP version. She concluded with this revolutionary advice:

> If the journalistic powers-that-be really care whether the news is read and digested, as opposed to merely being circulated, they can insist that logical organization and explicit connectives be the most important determinants of the story's form, and that sentence length, "human interest," and the editor's convenience be considered of less importance. And they can ask text-writers to kill the advice that quotes and colorful details "brighten up" a story; when included for that purpose, they are more likely to attract attention to

themselves and away from the news point of the story, and reduce the story to a jumbled collection of facts. Instead of teaching reporters cheap tricks to hide a multitude of flaws, instruction should concentrate on highlighting and enhancing whatever natural structure inheres in a story; the important question to ask about a story should not be "Is it flashy (or zippy or vivid) enough?" but "Is this a logically structured account?" And the key to writing good sentences within a story should not be "Are they short enough?" but "Is it going to be clear to the reader what the relevance of this information is, what the point of including it is?"[20]

Another insight into why the demands of modern reading are confounding many Americans has been offered by E. D. Hirsch of the University of Virginia. His 1987 book, *Cultural Literacy*,[21] ironically was trivialized by many newspapers, which published feature-page quizzes of the terms the book says culturally literate readers should know.

In the substance of the book, however, Hirsch argues that many people don't read because they don't have the "world knowledge" or "network of information that all competent readers possess." That is not to say that readers are ignorant; in fact, they know a lot, young people especially. But because of undemanding curricula in contemporary schools, what they know tends to be narrow, limited to their own generation, interest, or experience. And the shared knowledge—which newspapers assume their readers have—grows more and more complex and technical. For example, Hirsch cites research showing that

two-thirds of our seventeen-year-olds do not know that the Civil War occurred between 1850 and 1900. Three-quarters do not know what "reconstruction" means. Half do not know the meaning of "Brown decision" and cannot identify either Stalin or Churchill. . . . Moreover, our seventeen-year-olds have little sense of geography or the relative chronology of major events.

Others have found similar ignorance about science[22] and economics.[23]

How are these would-be readers to make sense of the newspaper? When they pick up a paper and collide with alien terms without which the stories have little meaning—Bosnia-Herzegovina, appeals court, zoning board, Dow Jones Industrial Average, House-Senate conference committee, genetic engineering—how can we expect them to be readers?

Journalists like to cite Thomas Jefferson's quotation about the importance of the press to democracy: "Were it left to me to decide whether we should have a government without newspapers, or newspapers without a government, I should not hesitate a moment to prefer the latter." Hirsch points out the rest of the quote: "But I should mean that every man should receive those papers and be capable of reading them."

The Disappearing Audience

When the Gallup poll reports that the proportion of Americans who admit having read no books in the past year doubled to 16 percent from 1978 to 1990, some see an ominous decline in reading generally. But they have to account for dramatic increases in the number of books published and sold (even if many of the titles are romance and mystery pulps), greater use of public libraries, and an explosion in the number and variety of magazines published.[24]

In fact, even the newspaper is holding its own—on Sunday. Between 1970 and 1991, the number of Sunday newspapers jumped from 586 to 875, Sunday circulation increased from 49.2 million to 62.1 million, and readership went from 91.6 million to 123 million. While the percentage of American adults who read the Sunday paper decreased until 1986, it rose again, reaching 67 percent by 1989 and holding steady since then.[25] Even with the intimidating bulk of the Sunday newspaper, people seem to find the time to read on that day of leisure.

The convergence of issues in Americans' motivation, opportunity, and ability to read a newspaper is starkly reflected in circulation (that is, copies sold) and actual readership on the busy, pressurized weekdays. Where once the typical citizen routinely began the day with the newspaper at the breakfast table or ended it with the evening paper after dinner—or both—today the harried worker may glance at someone else's sports page during the lunch break, or may not.

The routine, for many people, is broken. "What has changed is the strength of the habit of reading a newspaper," Albert E. Gollin, vice president and research director for the Newspaper Association of America, said. "It used to be one of those things that almost everybody did."[26]

So while the U.S. population grew approximately 30 percent from 1965 to 1991, daily newspaper circulation was flat. In the past twenty years, according to the Simmons Market Research Bureau, the proportion of adults who say they read a daily newspaper "yesterday" has fallen from 78 percent in 1970 to 62 percent in 1991. One ray of optimism is that the steepest fall was during the 1970s; the decline during the early 1980s was about a percentage point per year, and the 1991 figure of 62 percent was only a point less than in 1986. It is conceivable that readership is stabilizing.

But the demographics are not encouraging. Newspapers' loyal readers continue to be older, more affluent, better educated. Women and minorities are less likely to read the paper, and of course, the biggest concern is the young. Last year, only 30 percent of Americans under the age of thirty-five reported they had read a newspaper "yesterday," compared to 67 percent in 1965, according to a Times Mirror survey. The magazine *News Inc.* reported in 1992 that only 27 percent of eighteen- to thirty-four-year-olds read a newspaper every day, and they spent only twenty-three minutes doing it, compared to 239 minutes watching television. The National Opinion Research Center measured everyday readership and found substantial differences by age: 71 percent for those sixty and over, 59 percent for ages forty-five to fifty-nine, 47 percent for ages thirty to forty-four, and 28 percent for ages eighteen to twenty-nine. In 1973–75, those percentages were considerably higher: 48 percent of eighteen- to twenty-nine-year-olds were everyday readers then.

As ominous as they are, demographics are not the only readership issues, Gollin points out. Reading frequency has changed, with many people going from a seven-day, home-delivery subscription to occasional, or intermittent, single-copy purchases. "Baby boomers (born 1946–64) and post-boomers, beneficiaries of growing media diversity and lifestyle options, have turned out to be more selective newspaper readers," Gollin wrote.[27] They may buy the Wednesday paper for the food section, the Friday paper for the entertainment section, the Saturday paper for sports.

Similarly, Gollin points out, reading *styles* have changed. Where once a reader settled in and, as much for pleasure as anything else, "read the newspaper" from cover to cover, today a reader might seek out specific content and discard the rest of the paper. Simmons research shows that readers who look at every page have decreased from 62 percent in 1979 to 56 percent in 1991, while those seeking out only certain parts of the paper have increased from 38 percent to 44 percent, heavily weighted with young people. Gollin attributes this change to generational differences and the segmentation of newspaper content, but motivation/opportunity/ability issues surely have their own impact.

The New Economics of the Newspaper

A serious consideration of newspaper readership issues and the future of newspaper journalism must be within the context of a larger, even more threatening sea change—the weakening of the newspaper business itself.

Newspapers—which are, after all, businesses—have two kinds of customers: readers and advertisers. Certainly, flat circulation numbers hurt revenue, even when cover prices shoot up to 50 cents and home-delivery rate increases almost keep pace. But circulation income is only 15 to 20 percent of a newspaper's total revenue. The big dollars are in advertising.

As household penetration slid during the 1970s and 1980s—"graphs you could ski down," as one analyst graphically put it—the biggest fear for publishers was not so much the loss of readers as the loss of the advertising audience. Some papers fell below 60 percent penetration in their primary markets; a dip below 50 percent, and the ad salesperson no longer would be able to promise the all-important saturation or "mass coverage" to an advertiser.

Then, suddenly, as the 1980s ended and the 1990s began, that didn't much matter anyway. Newspapers, already off balance from the readership losses, were staggered by the combined force of three body blows.

One was the national recession. For more than a decade, total advertising spending had increased faster than the GNP, but it increased only 5 percent in 1989 and 3.8 percent in 1990, and headed lower as the recession deepened. As with previous recessions, newspapers began their participation earlier than other businesses, and they could have expected to pull out sooner, but for the other blows.

The second one was the shakeout—some would say upheaval—in retailing across the nation. Discounters, as exemplified by Sam Walton's Wal-Mart, suddenly were everywhere and everything. Traditional full-service department stores found themselves awash in merchandise and employees but bereft of customers. Local department stores traditionally lead retail display advertising, which usually accounts for half of newspaper ad revenue. But at one point in 1992, *USA Today* reported, companies with 24 percent of department store square footage were in Chapter 11 bankruptcy proceedings. Many discounters, such as Sam's Wholesale Club, don't advertise much, "passing on the savings to you."

But even with all that, the worst blow to newspapers probably was the third factor: the massive transition from repetitive, mass-circulation advertising toward what marketers believe are more cost-effective strategies. American consumers are bombarded with ads, commercials, and billboards—an average of three thousand advertising messages per adult per day. We ignore most of them and are cynical about many of the others. In 1986, 64 percent of adults could name a television commercial they had seen in the previous four weeks, according to surveys by Video Storybook Tests; by 1990, that had fallen to 48 percent.

Such questions about advertising effectiveness have led to a major, ongoing shift from advertising to promotion, in which advertisers forsake blind, mass exhortations in favor of coupons, sweepstakes, rebates, sales incentives, and the like—marketing tactics that have a more immediate, direct payoff and that do not rely nearly as much on expensive mass media like newspapers. Donnelley Marketing says companies now devote 70 percent of their marketing budgets to promotion and 30 percent to ads, compared to a 57:43 ratio a decade ago.

The newest strategy threatening newspapers consists of target, data-base, or direct marketing—all related terms. Targeting reflects advertisers' discovery that they may be wasting many of the dollars spent on mass media because they can narrow their reach to the people most likely to be their customers. For example, if a grocery store draws primarily from a five-mile radius, why should it pay to advertise in a newspaper that circulates across seven counties? For years, many newspapers have responded by offering ad space that can be changed by geography, but this zoning tended to be crude.

Crude, that is, compared to data-base marketing, a phenomenon made possible by modern computers and sophisticated software. It has revolutionized direct marketing—that is, reaching a specific, known customer. The data base has allowed marketers to accumulate information about customers and potential customers from many sources, so they know where people shop, the size and make-up of their family, their income, the cars they drive, their media habits, the products they buy, their hobbies and activities, their school and organizational ties, and even their psychographics—approximate (and questionable) projections of life-style types. Thus, companies can ask the computer for a list of twenty-five- to thirty-four-year-old, college-educated, white-collar Midwesterners with families who bought a minivan five to seven years ago and thus might be ready for a new one. For example, *Business Week* reported that Chrysler mailed a videocassette about its 1991 minivans to 400,000 current minivan owners.

Data-base marketing is also powerful because of the marketer's ability to measure and evaluate response extremely accurately. When you redeem that coupon or return that form, the computer knows all and tells all, heightening the effectiveness of the next mailing. Marketers have found that targeting and direct appeals through sophisticated use of data bases can provide better results for less money than the hopeful publication of an ad across undifferentiated

parts of a mass audience in uncertain geography. Suddenly, newspapers seem rather old-fashioned.

Once, print media and advertising were practically synonymous.
Then radio, followed by television and billboards, bit off shares. More
recently, the yellow pages became seriously competitive (capturing
6.8 percent of total advertising in 1990), and direct mail exploded (18.2
percent in 1990). With all this new competition, newspapers' share of
total advertising has fallen, slowly but steadily, from 26.6 percent in
1982 to 24.9 in 1990. Even at the local level, newspapers' share has
fallen below 50 percent.[28]

In 1990, total amount of dollars spent on newspaper advertising
decreased from the previous year for the first time since 1970, one of
only a few such setbacks since World War II.

For the overwhelming majority of newspapers, local retail advertising is the primary source of revenue. Classified advertising, generally
the second biggest category, is far less volatile, moving up and down
predictably with the local economy. National advertising, such as for
cars and packaged goods, drained by television, magazines, direct
marketing, and promotions, has been declining for years, to the point
where it is a relatively minor factor for most newspapers.

The other significant category of advertising revenue is freestand-
ing inserts (FSIs), which have become a very visible part of the modern
daily newspaper. Whether they are cents-off coupons, monochrome
Everything-on-Sale! fliers, or slick, full-color department-store catalogs,
FSIs have become an important component of newspaper economics.
To some readers, they may be as irritating as blow-in cards in magazines, or they may be important shopping information (many editors
have had their egos punctured by subscribers who cancel because they
don't get all the advertising inserts). To publishers, FSIs are a bitter-
sweet source of revenue: While they are low-cost, high-margin products, they represent advertising that once was ROP (run of press), the
expensive ads that bulked up the newspaper proper, supporting the
journalism, bonding the advertiser, and creating that information synergy that for so long was a part of most Americans' daily lives.

To advertisers, FSIs transformed the daily newspaper into a mere
delivery wrapper. Certainly, some value is associated with delivery in
a newspaper, of which the purchase proves the reader's interest. But
for some advertisers, delivery is delivery, whether the message is
tucked inside a newspaper wrapper or wedged in a screen door or
mailed. And advertisers often, or even usually, don't want their FSIs
delivered to a paper's entire readership; they want only certain, carefully selected segments. Newspapers are being forced to zone delivery

of inserts more and more narrowly, certainly by zip code and even by city block. As this zoning becomes more specific, the excluded areas represent lost revenue and irritated readers.

In 1991, one newspaper ad director ruefully recalled the years when his job was merely to schedule all those full-page units and raise rates every year, while the advertisers were expected to prepare their own ads, deliver them to the paper in the proper form and on time, and pay promptly. Suddenly, just to scratch out any sort of revenue uptwitch, he was having to cultivate small advertisers again, worry about the frequency and distribution of those insulting inserts, justify rate increases against flat circulation, comfort salespeople who couldn't make their commissions anymore, and worry about whether those weekday papers ever again would be hefty.

The Fuel of Democracy

So what? Who cares? Times are changing, technology is changing, and people are changing. We don't get our entertainment or food the way we once did; we don't live in the same family units we once did; we don't work or communicate the way we once did. Why should we get our news and information the way we did a hundred years ago? It is almost the turn of the century, after all, and we have computers, with modems, and we have fax machines and CNN and dozens of other television channels, soon to be interactive with everyone through fiber optics. The whole notion of cutting down a tree to make paper, using petroleum to make ink, a reporter's taking notes in longhand in an old-fashioned notebook, trying to fit it all on an oversized sheet of paper within a few hours, and then entrusting this awkward, inky thing to a twelve-year-old to carry to your house before dawn in a foot of snow—is that the best we can do in the twenty-first century?

Who makes slide rules anymore? Or typewriters? Horse-drawn plows? Egg beaters? Maybe newspapers are just another relic, with little remaining value save nostalgia.

In fact, newspapers serve at least two unique roles in our society and our democracy for which there is no new-technology successor. One is the contribution newspapers make to our collective intellect; the other is journalism.

Societal Intellect

The daily *Bugle* needn't be particularly "intellectual" to serve the intellect—that is, the capacity for knowledge and for rational and intelligent thought, the definition Neil Postman uses in his frightening book *Amusing Ourselves to Death*.[29] Postman, a communications theorist, says humankind is in the fourth era of communication (orality, writing, printing, and television). The evolution was natural and progressive until the last transition, when communication changed from the printed word to television.

Tracing social communication through American history, Postman points out that the United States was founded by intellectuals, an intelligentsia who read and wrote. Books were widely available, and public discourse and public business were based on the written word. Early Americans—of all kinds, in "a thriving, classless reading culture"—communicated, and thought, through writing. It is the nature of writing, he argues, to have content:

> Whenever language is the principal medium of communication—especially language controlled by the rigors of print—an idea, a fact, a claim is the inevitable result. . . . [I]t is very hard to say nothing when employing a written English sentence. . . . If a sentence refuses to issue forth a fact, a request, a question, an assertion, an explanation, it is nonsense, a mere grammatical shell. . . .[M]eaning demands to be understood. A written sentence calls upon its author to say something, upon its reader to know the import of what is said. And when an author and reader are struggling with semantic meaning, they are engaged in the most serious challenge to the intellect. [30]

So, Postman says, reading is an essentially rational activity, requiring linear thinking, logic, the understanding of questions, the hearing of answers, creating and assessing one's own contributions to the process. It is "mindwork," an exercise that causes the owner of the mind to learn and grow.

Television communicates far differently from the printed word. It does not require the active involvement of the viewer. It communicates largely through visual and aural imagery, not a logical, thoughtful sequence of words. The viewer absorbs the images almost by osmosis. The average length of a shot on network television is said to be 3.5 seconds; so the eye never rests, always having a new stimulus. Even the infamous sound bites are faster these days; one study found the average network news sound bite fell from forty-two seconds in 1968 to nine seconds in 1988. Despite media concerns and promises, sound bites averaged only 9.65 seconds during the 1992 campaign, and a dismal

9.01 seconds from September to November.[31] What all this means is that the viewer's mind is never allowed to pause to reflect, consider, think, or digest. One might say that commercial television tends to trivialize the most serious and important of subjects.

In a speech to newspaper publishers, Bob Pittman, the founder of MTV, talked about the secret of his invention. It was not the content of the music, he said, but the combination of the music, the visual images of the performers, and the action on the music videos. MTV has much in common with the television show "Miami Vice," which was at the height of popular culture at the time Pittman spoke. On close examination, one can see that the plot of "Miami Vice" was traditional, predictable cops-and-robbers. What made the show so popular was not its content, but an intense combination of rock music, highly stylized art direction that color-coordinated everything from clothes to cars, and images of drugs, violence, and sex. One did not think about "Miami Vice" or try to solve the mystery; one simply absorbed the images.

"The problem," Postman says, "is not that television presents us with entertaining subject matter but that all subject matter is presented as entertaining. . . . Thinking does not play well on television." [32]

As an example of the difference between discourse by writing and discourse by image, consider Postman's point about early American public figures:

> [They] were known largely by their written words . . . not by their looks or even their oratory. It is quite likely that most of the first fifteen presidents of the United States would not have been recognized had they passed the average citizen in the street. . . . To think about those men was to think about what they had written, to judge them by their public positions, their arguments, their knowledge as codified in the printed word. You may get some sense of how we are separated from this kind of consciousness by thinking about any of our recent presidents . . . and what will come to your mind is an image, a picture of a face, most likely a face on a television screen. . . . Of words, almost nothing will come to mind. This is the difference between thinking in a word-centered culture and thinking in an image-centered culture.[33]

Should you think television news is different from MTV, consider this from Robert MacNeil of the "MacNeil/Lehrer NewsHour," generally considered one of the better news shows on television: The principle of television news, he has written, "is to keep everything brief, not to strain the attention of anyone but instead to provide constant stimulation through variety, novelty, action, and movement. You are required . . . to pay attention to no concept, no character and no problem for more than a few seconds at a time."[34] News shows, he wrote, are based on the notion that "bite-sized is best, that complexity must be avoided, that nuances are dispensable, that qualifications impede the simple message, that visual stimulation is a substitute for thought, and that verbal precision is an anachronism."

In Wisconsin, there is the phenomenon of barn fires. They may rarely get a mention in the next day's newspaper, because the loss of an abandoned barn is not especially newsworthy. But they may be headline news on television because the film can be visually striking, that is, entertaining to viewers. If the camera crew can't get to a fire in time, it isn't news on television either. Postman writes:

> The concept of truth is intimately linked to the biases of forms of expression. . . . As a culture moves from orality to writing to printing to televising, its ideas of truth move with it. . . . The form in which ideas are expressed affects what those ideas will be. . . . You cannot do political philosophy on television. . . . The public has adjusted to incoherence and been amused into indifference. . . . The decline of a print-based epistemology and the accompanying rise of a TV-based epistemology has had grave consequences for public life—we are getting sillier by the minute.[35]

We may get sillier yet. Jane M. Healy, an educational psychologist who wrote *Endangered Minds,* maintains that this new era in mass communication may be actually altering children's brains, and thus behaviors and growth, in subtle but critical ways. Culture changes brains physically, Healy says: "[E]xperience—what children do every day, the ways in which they think and respond to the world, what they learn, and the stimulae to which they decide to pay attention—shapes their brains. Not only does it change the ways in which the brain is used, . . . but it also causes physical alterations . . . in neural wiring systems,"[36] what is known as neural plasticity.

In effect, she says, use it or lose it. A healthy brain stimulates itself by active interaction with what it finds challenging and interesting in its environment. In the case of today's children, that means that part-time parents—because almost all parents are in the work force, including three-quarters of mothers with school-age children—have reduced the child's nurturing environment and interpersonal contact, leaving television as the child's surrogate parent. Healy discusses the importance of parents' talking to their children and of reading to them, particularly stories without pictures, because of the importance of understanding words alone as the main source of meaning.

Teachers complain more about students' diminished attention spans than any other characteristic, Healy says, and she ties that in large part to television. She points to some findings that television may overstimulate children, create passive withdrawal, cause attention and listening problems, and create a need for some sort of classroom "special effects" to keep kids' attention.

For one example, Healy writes:

> Studies sponsored by advertisers have suggested the best way to get viewers to pay attention to their messages is to capitalize on the brain's instinctive responses to danger. First, sudden close-ups, pans, and zooms are effective in alerting the brain because they violate its reflex need to maintain a predictable "personal space"—a certain distance between oneself and others. Second, salient features such as bright colors, quick movements or sudden noises get attention fast, since brains are programmed to be extremely sensitive to such changes that might signal danger.[37]

Some research suggests that children thus stimulated might develop overactivity, frustration, irritability, and attention disorders. Healy cites a review of the few studies available indicating that prolonged television viewing might cause a syndrome of mental inactivity that would interfere with thinking or concentrating.

In an interview on Wisconsin Public Radio, Healy said television and, especially, video games can be psychologically addictive, keeping children from ever having what she called "a quiet mind." She said, "We need kids who can think."

A 1992 study by the Educational Testing Service found that kids who watch more television have lower test scores, and those who read more have higher test scores. The correlations, of data from previous surveys and tests, were so strong they "surprised even researchers who had seen these numbers individually before," according to *USA Today*. For example, eighth-graders in North Dakota read more at home than those in any other state, and they also scored highest among the thirty-seven states that used a national math achievement test. At the other extreme, District of Columbia eighth-graders watch the most television and read less than their peers in all but one other state, and they had the second worst math scores.[38]

Citing substantial evidence from other research and Scholastic Aptitude Test and Achievement Test scores, as well as anecdotes from educators, Healy says, hyperbolically: "The state of literacy in the United States today is declining so precipitously, while video and computer technologies are becoming so powerful, that the act of reading itself may well be on the way to obsolescence."

Journalism

Newspapers' other essential, and perhaps irreplaceable, role is journalism, the communitywide sharing of information and ideas that enables citizens to participate in their community relationships and governance. No other medium has shown an ability or willingness to provide the serious journalism necessary to fulfill the responsibilities of the First Amendment and serve the role of watchdog on government and other institutions capable of abusing their power over the people.

While television played a major role in ending the Vietnam War, it was not so much the information that television uncovered as it was the daily film it showed of Americans and Vietnamese fighting and dying. In contrast, the less visual Watergate and Iran-contra scandals might have gone unrevealed and unpunished except for the work, power, and persistence of newspapers.

Similar comparisons can be made at every level. What local television stations invest weeks and months of time and thousands of dollars to investigate official wrongdoing, as many local newspapers routinely do? For just one example, at my midsized daily newspaper: When Indian treaty rights to some natural resources erupted into political controversy and physical violence, the *Wisconsin State Journal* committed eighteen reporters, editors, and photographers to the story for various periods over four months, rented a house in the treaty territory, and sent staff to four other states, from Maine to Washington State to Oklahoma. What local television station would have made such an investment? We believe our work in investigation and public education had a significant impact on the progress made that year in the relations between Indians, whites, and the government. Television's contribution was to send its crews up to the Indians' boat landings in hopes of getting sensational film of racial violence.

But the journalistic value of newspapers is not just major reporting projects. Day in and day out, newspaper reporters are sitting in on school-board meetings and poking into city hall files and picking apart the records of political candidates—the real grist of journalism's primary job of keeping government honest, responsive, and off our backs. Government aside, it is the local newspaper that goes out and gathers the news of human activity, evaluates and digests it, and reports it.

Local television and radio stations commonly get most of their news off the wire and out of the newspaper, just adding video or audio tape to suit the medium. The electronic media can deliver the news first, but only if they know about it. A local television station's news staff might be a quarter of the size of the local newspaper's; maybe a third of them would be the all-important camera operators. As a young reporter on an afternoon paper, I heard my stories read—word for word, phrase for phrase—over the radio the next morning. During the 1992 campaign, Governor Mario Cuomo of New York told a group of newspaper editors they must take the lead in educating the electorate: "Television has to do it, but television won't do it unless you write it."

Without newspapers, who would gather the news, challenge the authorities, and accept the affirmative responsibility of the First Amendment, as opposed to merely standing behind it for self-serving reasons?

If much of the news on television already has been in the newspaper, why don't more people notice the duplication? One might conclude that all those television viewers out there just don't read their newspapers anymore, or maybe that—contrary to journalists' belief—they don't much care who has a story first.

In fact, it seems that television isn't delivering much news. For more than a quarter century, Americans have *said* they get most of their news from television, but in their book *The Main Source* [39] John P. Robinson and Mark R. Levy of the University of Maryland argue that is a false perception: "Television news should not be considered the public's main source of news." Viewers may *think* they get a lot of news from television because they watch a lot of television entertainment, but more Americans read a newspaper on a typical day than watch any television newscast, and spend more time doing it. As important, Robinson and Levy cite research showing that viewers really don't get that much news because of the limitations of television, including insufficient airtime to tell most stories; an easily distracted audience; the viewer's inability to control the pace of presentation; inadequate historical perspective, and inconsistencies between words and pictures. "[O]ne should not be surprised to find that much television news is beyond comprehension," they wrote, "when so few of its features were specifically designed to meet ordinary viewers' cognitive abilities and needs."

Anyone who thinks he or she absorbs much real information from the electronic media might try listening to an audiobook, that is, one read onto a tape cassette. That medium might be effective with a book of fiction, where the listener merely has to hear the rhythm of the words and follow a sequence of images and scenes. But on a recent long car trip, I tried to listen to Susan Faludi's *Backlash*, a nonfiction work full of statistics, citations, complex arguments, and rebuttals about the state of feminism. To process it all, one needs to compare numbers, check back to a first reference, organize the facts and arguments, and *see* how it holds together. Mimicking reading, I kept trying to replay sections of the tape as I drove and to take notes. Finally, I found myself having to be satisfied with major points, images.

As people continue to believe they are well informed by television, the failure of that medium to communicate comprehensible news will not, by itself, drive them back to newspapers. Robinson and Levy argue that word of mouth, just conversation, "may be at least as powerful a predictor of comprehension as exposure to news media." Without newspaper journalism, how would democracy function on a diet of rumor, gossip, hearsay, and the distortions of an endless chain of conversation?

The Future, Such as It May Be

Baltimore, Tulsa, Richmond, San Diego, Spokane, Dallas, Pittsburgh, Little Rock, Manchester, Baton Rouge, Union City, Shreveport, Lawton, Portland (Maine), Asheville, Newport News, Charleston, Durham, San Antonio, Gwinnett County (Georgia), Bethlehem, Anchorage—a death list of newspapers in the past two years. Generally, the loss has resulted from the merger of the afternoon paper into its morning partner or competitor. The explanation, time after time, is that the recession was the final blow to the longstanding decline in the afternoon reading habit, that the market no longer could support the costs of two operations, that instead of competing, the same resources could produce one newspaper superior to either of its predecessors.

But with the loss of each newspaper, the dribble of lost readers locally has become a spurt. Newspaper analyst John Morton has studied the merger of newspapers and found, "At best the surviving newspaper in the market can expect to capture about half the closed paper's circulation . . . 40 percent to 45 percent is the more common experience, and 30 percent to 35 percent has not been uncommon in failed-newspaper cities over the past ten years."[40] Duplicate readers account for some of the lost circulation, but there are too many newspaper dropouts.

Morton points out that most of the newspapers that have shut down since World War II were "blue-collar" newspapers, afternoon papers that served workers who went to their industrial jobs early in the morning and came home in the afternoon willing to read. There are fewer such workers in today's economy, and as they tend to be less educated than typical newspaper readers, they are more likely to break their already fragile relationship with newspaper reading and turn on the television.

Already, readership declines with each generation, and as the light-reading baby boomers replace today's heavy-reading seniors, it is not hard to imagine an information dichotomy. In the future, the vast majority of the citizenry might rely on the images of television and the vagaries of word of mouth for their understandings of their communities and the world, leaving an affluent, educated minority as newspaper readers, holding the power of information and knowledge, and creating a danger of the tyranny of the few.

In May 1991, as the newspaper economy reeled, the nation's publishers gathered for the annual American Newspaper Publishers Association (ANPA) convention and heard a depressing prognosis. For three years, ANPA's Competitive Analysis Project Task Force had been studying what new technology might do to the newspaper marketplace. As it turned out, the substance of the report had less to do with technology than with some painful decisions that newspapers soon may be required to make.[41]

The report was based on the possible demise of daily newspapers' traditional mission: delivering news and advertising of almost universal interest to a broad, reasonably interested audience. Both readers and advertisers had begun to fill their needs elsewhere. The task force saw four possible strategies for the newspaper:

The Mass Appeal. The newspaper would try to fill the diverse needs of a broad audience and keep market share by tightening its belt and constraining both advertising and circulation prices, with some sacrifice of profits.

The Class Appeal. Giving up on the mass readership, the newspaper would gear itself toward loyal, affluent, well-educated readers. Fewer readers paying higher prices would push penetration even lower, but advertisers would be asked to pay higher rates based on the upscale demographics. Profit margins would stay high.

The Individual Appeal. This strategy recognizes that the comprehensive newspaper cannot be all things to all people, that people have segmented themselves into groups with special interests. This newspaper would become a set of several, or many, newspapers targeted at major segments—for example, a stand-alone sports section, a business newspaper, extremely localized sections, a classified-advertising paper, demographically targeted weekly life-style papers. There would not necessarily be a general-news section. This approach would give both advertisers and readers exactly the products they say they want, and little more. It is a flexible, entrepreneurial strategy.

The Direct Appeal. The newspaper would direct its marketing to very specific market segments using a variety of techniques—including traditional ads and preprints but also telemarketing, audiotex, direct mail, alternate delivery to households, and more—in a total marketing package for local advertisers. One suggestion is an omnibus catalog of local merchants' wares. The operation would be based on an elaborate data base that begins with the newspaper's existing circulation lists but then is enhanced with other demographic and market data. This strategy is totally devoted to serving advertisers, and a newspaper would be merely one of the services if it remained profitable.

The Competitive Analysis Project (CAP) figured that, over the next ten years, these strategies would produce similar bottom lines, considerably short of the profit margins enjoyed by newspapers, at least until recently. Each would, however, leave the typical newspaper in a very different market position: The Class Appeal would give up circulation penetration for profits, the Mass Appeal would continue to rely heavily on those disappearing mass advertisers, and the Individual and Direct Appeals would rely on substantial investment in new products.

William B. Blankenburg, a professor of journalism at the University of Wisconsin–Madison applied industry data and trends to those four strategies for a peek into the future.[42] He suggested that, rather than alternatives, the four CAP strategies might be seen as "an evolutionary forecast," with a natural succession from the old Mass Appeal to a Class Appeal and then, as technology develops and competition changes, to a concentration on direct marketing.

Indeed, the industry seems to be headed in that direction. In the past few years, a number of newspapers have begun offering alternate delivery, that is, the use of circulation systems to deliver more than just the newspaper and its inserts. After all, the local newspaper is the only organization other than the postal service that visits, or at least passes, almost every house in the community every day. At my newspaper, the service is called Target Express and billed as offering the capability to deliver anything anywhere anytime in the circulation area, so long as it will fit in a newspaper tube. Candidates for the service include other newspapers—such as *USA Today* and the *New York Times*—magazines, shoppers, and even other-than-first-class mail.

Some newspapers are examining the feasibility of producing free-standing publications aimed at specific market segments, as in the Individual Appeal. In Wisconsin, there are in-depth weekly publications on the Green Bay Packers and the Wisconsin Badgers. The *Milwaukee Sentinel* is selling these special-interest newspapers by subscription through the mail and on newsstands. The *Grand Forks Herald* (North Dakota) began "Agweek," a weekly agribusiness section, as part of the newspaper but, when it recognized a separate market, spun it off as a separate publication. Undoubtedly, and quickly, there will be more to come as revenue-strained newspapers see market opportunities.

Many newspapers have bought into audiotex (information delivery by telephone), some to support their core business, others to preempt that technology as a source of future revenue. Newspaper executives are looking for partnerships, training, and opportunities for expanding, or moving, horizontally into the booming business of data-base marketing.

Where does all this leave the newspaper? Blankenburg concludes:

> If the evolutionary model is correct, the comprehensive daily newspaper is not viable. Only pieces of it will survive. . . . Some of its functions will be carried out by other means in the converged megamedium. The vertical integration of the newspaper industry will end, and with it, presumably, the local monopoly that owed to economics of scale in production. In the hazy future the optimist sees the public freed from the shackles of old monopolistic media that constricted the flow of information vital to democracy. But the pessimist worries that a huge information utility controlled by mammoth venal corporations will widen the gaps between rich and poor, invade privacy, and destroy the communities of interest that shared the comprehensive daily newspaper.[43]

Ever since American newspapers have stood on their own, apart from partisan subsidies of the early years, they have been schizophrenic:

on one side, journalism, gathering and delivering news and opinion, fueling the democracy; on the other side, commerce, conducting business on behalf of owners, with the responsibility of making profit. With some exceptions, such as the occasional tensions between the newsroom and aggrieved advertisers, the two roles have been mutually supportive or, at least, tolerant. Now the changes in life-style and the market are forcing the issue. To avoid what Theodore Levitt of Harvard Business School called "marketing myopia"—for example, the railroads thinking they were railroads rather than transportation companies and thus losing their markets—newspapers must become information-marketing companies. That immediately begs the question of whether their arsenal of strategies will include a commitment to journalism.

The Essence of the Newspaper

The issue of business versus journalism pivots on journalists' traditional belief that they really *are* the newspaper, that the commerce of the newspaper is potentially evil and intrusive (or at least threatening), that journalists are different from the rest of the world.

In fact, as society increasingly sees newspapers, and as journalists must begin to see themselves, the newspaper is no longer a household utility but has become a consumer product, and as a result, journalism becomes marketing of information, ideas, and attitude. The marketing perspective assumed in this discussion—with such concepts as MOA, industry life cycle, involvement, product substitution, marketing myopia—shows not only the propriety but also the necessity and value of journalists' opening their priesthood to the real world of real people with real needs and wants. To the consumer, the daily newspaper is just another expensive product of marginal personal value—and at that, one that every day demands a piece of his or her valuable time, money, and intellectual labor. While retaining the important principles of integrity, independence, and journalistic mission, newspapers should look at their markets and their product in much the same professional, methodical way that, say, Saturn conceived, researched, designed, produced, and marketed its new cars or Frito-Lay developed and tested O'Grady's potato chips. In truth, most journalists have about as much interest in data-base marketing as they do in the shoe business, but they must begin to look at the world as if they are selling something if they are to avoid having to do so in their next careers.

That is not to say that journalists should compromise their conviction that "newspapers," in some form, whether ink on paper or images on screen, are essential to democracy. This belief is based not only on the nature of reading and public discourse but also on the fact that only newspapers have succeeded at performing substantial, productive, effective journalism, particularly at the local level. In most cities and towns in this country, the loss of newspapers would mean there would be little "news," much less substantive, solution-oriented journalism. Prescriptions, such as the "mass versus class" choice from the Competitive Analysis Project, seem to ignore or gloss over the constitutional role of newspapers.

But newspapers, whatever their higher mission, must compete and survive in the free market.

Reinventing, or reviving, the newspaper will require a transformation of attitude among newspaper people, a creative melding of their traditional altruism and a new pragmatism. We must not abandon our idealism, romance, and philosophy, but rather make them our color guard. The front line must be a passion and ability to compete in the marketplace of time, interest, and value. To begin with, journalists must move beyond their storied defensiveness: Why don't readers know how good and important newspapers are? What's wrong with *them*?

Then newspapers must resist superficial, easy solutions. Perhaps for lack of any better ideas, the defensive fads in the industry (which Howard Kurtz details in the accompanying paper) have been inspired by what are seen as competitors. If radio is faster than print, well, just add more immediacy to the front pages, and sharpen the headline verbs. If people watch a lot of television and television is visual and colorful, then use more pictures and lots of color. If young people are more visual and less literate these days, let's give them informational graphics and youth-oriented personalities. *USA Today*'s newsracks even look like television sets! But newspapers are not television or radio, and cannot be.

While downsizing or "rightsizing" has become a buzzword, we must remember that mindless cost cutting at the expense of product or quality is selling out the future. Research shows that better newspapers, with more resources, perform better in the marketplace.[44] Just as we tell advertisers that down periods are when they should intensify advertising, this time of change and danger is the time for newspaper companies to invest in their products. If customers demand more and better content, we would be foolish to deny them. That, however, is not to advocate throwing money at traditional newsrooms or newsprint suppliers; now also is the time for publishers to demand accountability from editors, to be shown that the money is being well spent in pursuit of the newspaper's mission and the company's goals.

Among the new attitudes must be the acceptance of change as normal, continuous, and eternal. Journalists often are resistant to new ways of thinking about and practicing their profession. Many reporters and editors still had beat-up Underwood typewriters, paste pots, and Linotype machines well into the 1970s and even the 1980s. When newsrooms grudgingly accepted computers, at least one programmed the computers to end stories with a command of "-30-," the traditional signoff. And if finally forced to change, journalists will resist anything that smells of commercialism: We certainly don't have customers; we have readers. We don't acknowledge the existence of a market; it is a circulation area. We would never produce a product; it is a newspaper or a section or a column. Even with all their implications, such semantics are trivial compared to newspaper journalists' view of the outside world. Might anyone else, even readers, ever tell newspapers how to do journalism? Heresy!

The new newspaper will lead a process of change, response, and adaptation that probably will never end. As technology and our readers change, so will we.

Much of the fearfulness about the fate of newspapers grows out of revolutionary technology. While newspapers likely will continue in their current technological state into the twenty-first century, at some point inevitably will come a great leap into more efficient technology: a screen in every home, with a laser printer for those who still want portability. Roger Fidler, who works on new media technology for Knight-Ridder Inc., foresees, within five years, a thin, flat, tablet-sized, portable computer that will offer an electronic newspaper, complete with video on demand, exhaustive choices, and interactive ads.[45]

But the microchip does not mean the death of reading; it will mean change in the delivery and, perhaps, the act of reading. Historian Daniel Boorstin, citing a "displacement fallacy," has pointed out that, contrary to some expectations, radio not only survived television, but even prospered in a new role: "New technologies tend to discover unique opportunities for the old."[46]

We must not confuse the physical delivery of journalism with its substance. New technologies will emerge, and their significance will be less than the survival of the essence of the newspaper, the content. The value of the newspaper, regardless of its form, is in the message: the thinking, planning, gathering, writing, editing, selecting, and presenting of information and ideas—and, on the receiving end, the reading and comprehension.

Revitalizing the essence of the newspaper will require disciplines previously alien to a profession whose image, public and self, has been a romantic combination of iconoclast, social worker, devil's advocate, watchdog, troublemaker, poet, and swaggering bounty hunter. Now we must become methodical, purposeful—one might even say businesslike.

If journalists need a shove to think of their institution in a businesslike way, they might look at it as a businessperson does. Consider the cold perspective of investor Warren Buffett, chairman of Berkshire Hathaway. Buffett, burdened not by being a journalist but by heading a company with significant newspaper holdings, wrote in an annual report letter to shareholders that media properties, in their "economic behavior," have begun to resemble *businesses* more than *franchises:*

> An economic franchise arises from a product or service that (1) is needed or desired, (2) is thought by its customers to have no close substitute, and (3) is not subject to price regulation. The existence of all three conditions will be demonstrated by a company's ability to regularly price its product or service aggressively and thereby to earn high rates of return on capital. Moreover, franchises can tolerate mismanagement. Inept managers may diminish a franchise's profitability, but they cannot inflict mortal damage. In contrast, a "business" earns exceptional profits only if it is the low-cost operator or if supply of its product or service is tight. Tightness in supply usually does not last long. . . . And a business, unlike a franchise, can be killed by poor management. Until recently, media properties possessed the three characteristics of a franchise and consequently could both price aggressively and be managed loosely. Now, however, consumers looking for information and entertainment . . . enjoy greatly broadened choices as to where to find them. Unfortunately, demand can't expand in response to this new supply: five hundred million American eyeballs and a twenty-four-hour day are all that's available. The result is that competition has intensified, markets have fragmented, and the media industry has lost some—though far from all—of its franchise strength.[47]

Buffett's hard economic assessment makes "marketing" sound almost altruistic, eh? But as newspapers evolved into bigger businesses and, commonly, subsidiaries of large, publicly traded media companies, they became subject to the same demanding business standards of any other commodity. In their hearts, such Buffetts personally may love newspapers—he is, after all, in his sixties—but in their heads, they realize the traditional news business is falling short on the earnings-growth report.

Marketing approaches—in which an enterprise endeavors to satisfy the wants and needs of consumers—have been discussed in the newspaper business since the 1970s, primarily as a philosophy and structure for unified, or at least cooperative, functioning of the advertising, circulation, and promotion departments, sometimes under one marketing director or vice president. Journalists scoffed at the very thought, insisting that commercial concerns should not interfere with the standards and instincts central to what we have considered our profession. At times, when some used "marketing" as a euphemism for pandering to the baser interests of some readers, disdain was justified. To the newsroom, marketing became what happened after the pages were composed.

The argument in this paper is that editors can learn from and adapt the marketing concept, and use marketing knowledge and techniques, without compromising the independence, integrity, and instinct that make newspapers what they have been, and should remain. Marketing can, and does, do good.

The newspaper must consciously separate its constitutional mission from its market strategies and tactics. While the guiding spirit will be the former, the newspaper will survive and prosper, if it does, on its value in the marketplace—the value of its ideas and journalism certainly, but in a more immediate sense, the paper's simple value in the reader's life. Newspapers have to earn their way, create and deliver value, and accomplish measurably worthwhile things, just like everything and everyone else in the marketplace.

In fact, if high-minded journalists need a rationale for beginning to think in marketing frameworks, they might feel most comfortable in the branch of marketing called social marketing. Among its definitions is this one: The use of marketing knowledge and techniques in the dissemination of products or services for prosocial reasons, that is, reasons other than profit alone.

The newspaper's aim is to cause more people to read more often, not only for its financial independence and success, but also for the good of society. Whether a stockholder and an editor put different relative weights on those outcomes does not matter. The purpose, and passion, need be no less intense.

A conscientious editor, for example, will be greatly concerned about falling readership among low-income people, to whom the subscription price—as much as $200 a year—undoubtedly is a consideration. While many publishers seem to think circulation eventually rebounds completely after the price goes up, there is evidence that, with each incremental increase, another segment of potential readership is lost or, at least, discouraged.[48] One solution worth trying could be tiered pricing, with lower-cost subscriptions offered in low-income neighborhoods. Under circulation-auditing standards, subscriptions discounted as much as 50 percent still can be counted into the advertising base, and even at that discount, the subscription still makes money. So the stockholder gets the profit, and the editor gets the reader.

The Marketing of Newspaper Journalism

A marketing approach to newspaper journalism should be based on finding, or creating, a consumer need or want that newspapers *uniquely* can fill, then filling it. Newspaper people must free themselves from useless constraints of tradition and become more thoughtful, analytical, professional, realistic, methodical, and open-minded about their . . . product.

Contrary to popular belief, marketing does not mean mere selling, but encompasses the entire process, from idea through aftermarket, based on the marketing mix, or four P's: product, price, promotion, and place (distribution).

For example, Leo Bogart, who studied newspapers for more than twenty years at the Newspaper Advertising Bureau, helping lead its intensive 1977–83 Newspaper Readership Project, concluded that "the really critical steps required to reestablish the position of newspapers as a universal mass medium involve distribution and not content." In 1981, he called for measures to advance the efficiency of newspapers' distribution system by further professionalizing circulation personnel and upgrading their status within the organization and also by improving the mechanics and systems through which papers are sold, paid for, and physically handled and through which subscribers' demands and complaints are handled.[49]

In fact, distribution—long a second thought, relegated to the hands of an army of willing kids—is currently at the forefront of industry attention, thanks in part to targeted advertising inserts and alternate delivery. The kids have become too hard to recruit and too expensive, and they are being replaced by corps of adults who can cover much larger routes in their cars. According to the International Circulation Managers Association, the number of under-eighteen carriers plummeted from 823,746, or 90 percent of all carriers, in 1980, to 362,470, or 66 percent, in 1990. When the Pittsburgh newspapers dismissed all their 4,300 young carriers in 1992, a spokesperson said, "We can't stay in business trying to stay with a tradition that has outlived its usefulness."[50] The future of distribution, of course, is electronic and, again, coming at its own pace.

But the most reliable delivery imaginable will not make a reader out of someone without the motivation, opportunity, and ability to read the newspaper. One might see those questions in the light of the other two P's: price—in time as well as money—and product—represented by self-interest and ability to read. What can the marketing concept mean to these most personal of newspaper readership issues?

The Need for Research

To begin with, we need to know more. Other manufacturers of consumer products invest heavily in survey research, focus groups, product development, market testing, and postpurchase feedback. Research and development always have been rare in the newspaper industry, and recent examples—such as the development of *USA Today* and Knight-Ridder's Boca Raton *News*, described by Howard Kurtz in his paper—stand out as exceptions rather than precursors. The industry is beginning to support such efforts as New Directions for News, a think tank for creativity based at the University of Missouri.

But experience, instinct, and tradition—or habit—are still the principal tools editors use to decide what to cover, how to cover it, how to write and package the coverage, and the myriad other factors that constitute the daily newspaper. There is an impressive body of readership research, much of it proprietary, but it tends to be limited to descriptive survey research, profiling readers and nonreaders and exploring how people say they use media and what they like and dislike in newspapers. Rarely is it prescriptive, given people's inability to say what new ingredients might bond them to newspaper reading. [51]

Newspapers need insight and ideas. One potential framework could be the motivation/opportunity/ability model, going beyond the immediate question of newspaper reading and examining people's life-styles, needs, and preferences. We know people will and do read; we do not know what we must do to inspire them to need and read newspapers regularly. Answers will come not so much by asking people but by creatively probing and experimenting. In addition to quantitative survey methods, researchers in consumer behavior, a branch of marketing, are developing qualitative, interpretive research techniques that allow exploration of phenomena beyond simple answers to one- or two-dimensional questions. We may find such approaches necessary because newspapers and their readers are complex beings who apparently interact in labyrinthine ways at several levels.

For example, at the *Wisconsin State Journal* we avoided a potentially serious mistake by going beyond the traditional random survey of readers to gauge possible reaction to the proposed condensing of printed financial listings. After that study found out how many people used which listings how often and other such straightforward information, we performed some qualitative research, using a depth-interview technique to explore what benefits readers received from the listings and how these benefits related to their personal needs and values. It turned out that few readers use the listings to actually trade stocks. Instead, they use them for a variety of unforeseen purposes. One man checked not only his own stocks but also his friends' investments, so they would have something to talk about during golf. Another liked to check stocks he had sold years before, to reassure himself he had made the right decision. But the most striking was my interview with a woman who had invested an inheritance in stocks she said she never would sell. She checked their prices every day just to be sure her late grandmother's money was secure. To her, the investments are more like an heirloom than an asset, and the stock listings are a sort of link to her ancestors. Given such insights, the listings were not condensed.

Newspapers need more controlled, measured experimentation, particularly at the micro level where people interact with the content. ASNE's Literacy Committee (which I chair), along with the Poynter Institute and the University of Wisconsin–Madison, are analyzing results of an experiment—on deadline at the *St. Petersburg Times*—to test different reporting and writing techniques on random samples of readers. The goal is to see whether innovative or, at least, nontraditional techniques will help to bring aliterates back to the newspaper.

Without regard to the results, that experiment is noteworthy because of the collaboration—between newspaper professionals and academics. In other fields, such as marketing, the role of academia is not only to train practitioners but also to do research in support of their practice. Industry commonly supports such scholars and their research. One can pick up a copy of the *Journal of Consumer Research* or the *Journal of Marketing* and read substantive articles about solid research into small, arcane, but potentially important corners of marketing knowledge.

Where is this collaboration in journalism? The best journalism schools are traditionally divided between the craft training of reporters and editors on one side and, on the other, what practitioners derisively have called "communicologists," the Ph.D.'s who talk about theory and have no idea how to cover a fire. For their part, the mass-communications researchers seem to be more interested in the newer media, particularly the powerful television. Rarely do the two sides talk, much less collaborate, and there is little mutual respect.

Newspaper journalism no longer can afford to wing it. Hat in hand if necessary, journalists must prevail upon the universities and their best researchers to devote their considerable resources and knowledge to theory-based thinking and research on reading and newspapers. The argument has to be that, as important and interesting as television is, the stake here reaches beyond the future of newspapers to the future of our democracy.

The plea must come with money to support the research. This already has begun, with major grants from the Freedom Forum and the Knight Foundation, the latter having endowed chairs at journalism schools across the nation, including one for $1 million at the University of North Carolina at Chapel Hill for basic research on the future of newspapers. Newspaper companies should make similar investments, in theory-based research as well as applied research and development.

In addition to working with media theorists, newspapers also can learn to be quiet and listen to thinking and knowledge from other fields that may have applications in newspaper journalism. Newspapers can learn from marketing, which has made a science of understanding markets and the people in them; psychology and social psychology, which have knowledge of the wherewithal and attitudes the reader brings; literature, which knows more about writing; engineering, which might help with the ergonomics of newspapers; communication arts, which have a better understanding of how people really communicate.

Examples are throughout this discussion. Here are four more: The ASNE literacy experiment has some theoretical roots in work done on television soap operas by Sonia M. Livingstone of England. Her theory of interpretive resources offers a framework for examining the personal relationship between the reader and the words and perhaps bringing them closer together.[52] Psychology researchers recently have shown that people's "flight or fight" instincts lead them to pay more attention to negative than positive information, which could help us understand readers'—and thus newspapers'—love-hate relationship with bad news.[53] The *Wisconsin State Journal*'s reporter-beat reorganization—to focus more on reader interests and issues that cut across institutions and less on the institutions themselves—was inspired in part by William Paisley's classification of the social and behavioral sciences and how they cover their "beats."[54] A stream of research in advertising suggests that, in some circumstances, males and females process messages differently: Women tend to use a deeper, more substantial and detailed approach, while men more often use a quicker strategy based on pre-conceptions.[55] What might that mean to our male-dominated newspapers trying to stanch a loss of women readers?

Understanding the Newspaper's Competitive Advantages

In newspapers' frustration at the loss of their dominance, they tend to dwell on other media's advantages, leading to the more-color-and-shorter-stories syndrome of trying to compete on their turf. By focusing on the audience rather than on our problems, the marketing concept would lead us to build our strategies on *our* strengths, on what we, even with our quaint technology, uniquely can do for customers.

We have long enjoyed the power of newspapers without under-standing all the sources of the power. The daily newspaper is more than the sum of its parts; just watch a true reader organize and fold and sometimes almost caress the pages during his or her reading rit-ual. There was the woman at a *Detroit Free Press* focus group who, when asked what she liked in the paper, could not find the right words, but clutched the newspaper to her chest and averred: "This is my newspaper." And on a recent midweek Milwaukee-to-Washington flight, I watched a woman across from me devote every moment to absorbing my—her—Sunday *State Journal*, page by page, story by story, three days after it was published.

Newspapers have a synergy that gives them a life and power at the reader's emotional or feeling level that other media do not enjoy. The television relationship can be addictive; newspapers can be emotion-al as well as utilitarian. The intangibles that are competitive advan-tages must be studied and understood, so that they may be used affir-matively. "There are things about a newspaper that are attuned to the human spirit," Bill Baker, a Knight-Ridder vice president, has said, "and it'll be there forever."

What are newspapers' competitive advantages?

News. Walter Cronkite, himself a newspaper lover, liked to say that a typical television news show had less information in it than just the front page of a newspaper. Only the newspaper realistically can have truly comprehensive reporting of the important developments in the community, nation, and world. Newspapers should worry less about competing with television to have the headline first and, instead, develop their image as the primary source for details, explanation, insight and understanding, localization and personalization. People will hear the headline on radio and see the film on television, but they will have to get a newspaper to feed the appetite naturally created by major news. That does not mean just the space shuttle *Challenger*; editors who expand their conception of news will find broad and deep interest in breaking news stories most days, and developing news stories on the others. While letting television pique the interest, the key for newspapers is to be sure they satisfy it, answering all the reader's questions.

Importance. Through the drama of their sets and music and the deep tones of their voices, television anchors and reporters can sound like the source of all wisdom. This show business is not lost on viewers who also read newspapers. Television can bombard the public with images, but newspapers can make a difference in the substance of public affairs. While local investigative reporting seems to run in cycles, newspapers ought to realize this is one of their primary advantages. A newspaper should have at least one major reporting project under way all the time, not just on the obvious, crooked public officials, but on systems that don't work, problems that affect people, injustices that need righting. It may be that only newspapers have the wherewithal to take on these tough, demanding stories, and we should never let the public forget that. Through copyrights, promotion, and insistent, consistent follow-up, the newspaper must be sure readers know who made what happen, and who didn't.

Good Reading. The growing sales of books, for both adults and children, and the booming popularity of the thick Sunday newspaper indicate that many people simply enjoy reading. There is something deeply personal and warm about "curling up with a good book." Reading can be demanding for many people, as Neil Postman says, but even for them, it can be pleasurable. The act is quiet and solitary and tactile—one can touch the pages, read at one's own speed, scanning ahead or checking back, cogitating, savoring. Television is passive; one can feel objectified. Reading is active; there is a feeling of personal involvement and power. Aside from the functions of news and information, newspapers can serve this human pleasure and bond the reader to the medium. Every editor knows the emotional ties readers have with some columnists; the ASNE literacy experiment hopes to show such ties can be created throughout the newspaper. To capitalize on this advantage, the newspaper might find more, and better, uses for storytelling techniques.

Information Management. The information age is overwhelming Americans. Electronic media—the radio running in the car, the television as background noise at home—and print—newspapers, magazines, mailings, handouts—are everywhere in our days, invited or not. We are asked, implored, suggested, demanded, to consume, or at least consider, every bit of information someone has chosen to communicate. In his book *Information Anxiety,*[56]Richard Saul Wurman says, maybe apocryphally, "A weekday edition of the *New York Times* contains more information than the average person was likely to come across in a lifetime in seventeenth century England."

Almost any home would welcome a single, readily available, helpful, mostly comprehensive source of essential or useful information. By virtue of its handy technology, resources, and portability, the newspaper is best equipped to be this single source. The electronic media's weather forecast can help people choose their day's clothes, but—in this era at least—it really cannot handily deliver the school lunch menu, visually sort out and prioritize the news, provide details of road construction, list the sale prices of a number of products, or help pick a restaurant or a movie. Even if nothing else, the newspaper every day should be the best, most complete, most constructively critical guide to that day's television programming.

Wurman advises readers, "The secret to processing information is narrowing your field of information to that which is relevant to your life, i.e., making careful choices about what kind of information merits your time and attention. Decision making becomes more critical as the amount of information increases." Among Wurman's suggestions is for media consumers to critically evaluate their media, asking, among other things, "How does this story apply to my life?" Editors might well ask the same question: What will this story mean to readers? How can we make it mean more? What is the essential, relevant information they cannot get elsewhere? How can we help readers with this? Among their other perspectives, editors might look at the newspaper as an owner's manual for a reader's life.

Explanation. As information explodes, so does confusion. The world, even the community, changes faster and faster, with layer upon layer of social issue, technology, relationships, stresses. The newspaper can be a translator, making sense of the increasingly complex world. This competitive advantage can be realized as newspapers improve their writing and cultural literacy. On every major story, an editing point should be: What might a reader see as unclear in this situation? How can this story clarify it?

Community. While television may have become Americans' tribal campfire, the newspaper remains the community chronicler, the traditional wall on which banns are posted. Somehow, many occasions in our culture are not really recognized as important until they are in the newspaper. It is where we recognize achievements, honor heroes, announce engagements, report weddings, celebrate anniversaries, shame malefactors, and thank benefactors and samaritans. It is as if the newspaper holds the power of validation.

Editors learn the minimum level of recognition to be given a local high-school championship team, and they know clippings of honor rolls and civic clubs live forever in family scrapbooks. I remember the high-powered lawyer who steamed across a crowded room to tell me how angry he was at my newspaper. Since he also was a lobbyist, I assumed the issue was political, but that was not what was so important. His daughter had just graduated with considerable honors from Stanford, and he had been told the paper didn't have a regular place for such an item (we created one). There was the woman who routinely called me to demand coverage of crew regattas whenever one was in town. After several years of trying to satisfy her, it came out in one of our conversations that she only picked up the paper when she thought there would be a crew story. "I never have time to read the paper," she said merrily, but she believed firmly that the crew results were so important they should be there. Our family archives include several copies of one of my competitors' front pages, because my four-year-old was accidentally included in a feature photograph. Somehow, to us, the photo became special by our knowing it had been plopped on front porches all over town. Editors call this phenomenon "refrigerator journalism" because so many of those clippings end up behind magnets.

Once newspapers understand their competitive advantages, they can build on them, use them to leverage the market, and accomplish their larger missions. Instead of promoting subscription gimmicks and premiums, they can sell their journalism.

Wholism and Entrepreneurism

Newspapers have stepped away from the days, just a few years ago, when advertising salespeople were considered enemies of the newsroom and circulation was thought of as the department of truck drivers whose job it was to shut up and deliver. As jobs in those two areas have become so much more challenging and promising, newsrooms have come to view them with grudging respect.

The current, and future, difficulties demand far more than that. Newspapers need a new attitude of wholism, an understanding that their organic whole can be more than the sum of their separate functions. Most newspapers now coordinate their planning; the next step is to integrate it. The journalists—without any compromise of their independence, integrity, or mission—can work side by side with their advertising and circulation counterparts to find or develop markets they can serve, to their mutual benefit. The common goal simply is reaching readers, and it best can be accomplished through a new synergy among the three departments, respecting one another's sometimes disparate missions and capitalizing on one another's strength.

The wholism will cultivate entrepreneurism. Newsrooms traditionally have provided news or feature matter for advertising-driven special sections, but future teamwork must be much more substantial and interactive. Some of the marketing prescriptions call for targeting of substantial reader or advertiser segments, and true teamwork could find segments shared by significant portions of readers *and* advertisers. Geographic segments have been widely developed, through zoned "neighbors" sections. There remains great potential in thematic reader/advertiser segments, such as local business, sports, health care, and institutions like universities and major employers. While such new targeted efforts sometimes might cannibalize advertising and readership from the core newspaper, there should be not only new revenues and reader interest, but also a value-added dynamism in the overall newspaper. Progressive advertising and circulation departments are barreling into data-base marketing and alternate delivery, and if newsrooms are not to fall into second-class status, editors must begin to explore how these marketing phenomena can work, or at least coexist, with their journalism.

Farther out, but nearer every year, is the tailored newspaper, made possible by the coming technology. Readers will be able to customize their own newspapers by buying only the sections, or stories, of personal interest. Journalists should be worried that the selections will be so narrow that the dynamics, the serendipity, of the organic newspaper will be lost. Now, we rationalize publishing the horoscope and the comics, for example, by assuming that, on their way to those pages, some readers will be seduced by the stories about the federal budget deficit and the Middle East. If readers can choose just what they want, how many will choose the challenging opinion page, the deeper public-affairs coverage, the substance?

In their partnerships, journalists should begin working to ensure that their entrepreneurial new products revolve around the axle of their journalistic mission. If the newspaper company evolves into a comprehensive community information center, a model might be cable television: Customers start with the core product—the heart of the newspaper, with its journalism—then they can add on premium sections and services. Such a commitment on the part of modern media companies could mean stopping just before the short-term maximization of profits, but in the long run, who more than media companies will benefit from a literate, educated, informed, involved public?

Rebuilding the Base

The most abject pessimism, even fatalism, about the future of newspapers may be justified by a glance at readership figures clearly showing that the younger people are, the less they read newspapers. The trend line has been steadily down through the television era, though it seems to have slowed, or even leveled, in the 1980s. However, in a generational chart created by Al Gollin using National Opinion Research Center surveys, one can see a glimmer of hope. The chart shows fifteen years of readership by people born in specific eras, from Old Timers (born 1900–1914) through Late Boomers+ (born after 1959), with successively lower readership for each generation. "Contrary to the conventional wisdom, however," Gollin points out, "these findings strongly suggest that once newspaper readership habits are formed, probably by age thirty for most individuals, they tend to remain constant. Once the reading habit is established at some level of intensity, in other words, it lasts a lifetime."[57]

Newspapers must attract the young now if they are to have them as adults. For many years, newspapers have relied on Newspapers in Education (NIE), a program of furnishing newspapers to participating schools at reduced cost. The problem has been not only lukewarm support of NIE but also the larger question of, once youngsters have adult newspapers in their hands, what is there for them to read? While time may or may not be quite the factor with young people, there are still the issues of motivation and ability. Young people seem to be less comfortable reading, and E. D. Hirsch, the English professor who wrote *Cultural Literacy*, suggests that cultural literacy may be even lower among them. And, of course, there is the biggest disincentive for young readers: The typical newspaper contains very little content created for them. The news and features naturally assume a literate, involved adult who votes, works, pays taxes, and decides on such matters as whether the household subscribes to a newspaper.

This is beginning to change. A number of newspapers recently have created pages and sections targeted at young readers, and there are several new offerings from syndicates that can be used in newspapers anywhere. The Newspaper Association of America and the Children's Television Workshop are collaborating on one such program. While such efforts are encouraging, more needs to be done.

Again, we can learn from other, more professional marketers—perhaps the tobacco, alcohol, and athletic-shoe industries. In their apparent efforts to recruit young customers, cigarette and beer companies appeal to young people's desires to act like adults and achieve sociability, and the shoe companies play on social acceptance. Those are potential appeals for newspapers as well, but they have a tremendous advantage over the tobacco and alcohol industries: Their interest is prosocial and shared by the educators who have complete, guaranteed, structured access to youngsters from ages six to eighteen. Teachers are, or would be, allies, given their interest in reading, public affairs, and the democratic process. Chris Whittle's Channel One has met stiff resistance in its efforts to get into the schools because its commercial nature is inescapable, but what teacher would resist a responsible newspaper aimed at young readers?

That last phrase is key. Many young people—who do not yet vote or pay taxes and may not see a larger world beyond their own—are not going to be interested in an adult newspaper, much beyond comics and sports. Traditional youth pages have been written with adults-talking-to-kids style, emphasizing the value of school, the dangers of drugs, and the like. Is it any wonder such corners of the newspaper didn't exactly take root in the youth culture? In a research and development project for ASNE, the *Wisconsin State Journal* created a prototype section named "Rumpus," which attempted to be a newspaper by, for, and about young people, from their perspective. For one thing, it transcended the common assumption that kids are kids, whether they are seven or seventeen years old. Age groups are as different from each other as they are from adults, so "Rumpus" had segmented pages for five- to nine-year-olds, ten- to fourteen-year-olds, and fifteen- to eighteen-year-olds. Then the prototype tried to look at the world—their world, that is—from their perspective and cover news as they would define it. They were allowed to speak for themselves and ask their own questions, to which they got straightforward, as opposed to parental, answers. Recognizing that young people can read, "Rumpus" tried to give them a reason to. In testing the prototype with a random sample of at-risk and potential readers, researchers found a real generation gap reflecting different worldviews of adults and youngsters. For example, fifteen- to eighteen-year-olds were twice as likely as their parents to read a column by a local disc jockey and five times as likely to find value in it. Overall, adults said they would be more likely to read the newspaper if it included "Rumpus," and adults with children were even more positive. Young people showed strong reading interest in the features related to their own interests and experiences.[58]

Each newspaper should consider its own ambitious local program to reach young readers. It may well be that a weekly page is not enough to bond youngsters to the hassle of the newspaper. Because it is so different from newspapers' primary audience, this important segment may need its own newspaper, perhaps only weekly, but conceived, written, and edited for its unique readers. Kids themselves could, and should, do much of the newsgathering and even writing, with professional facilitation and resources. The natural partners, the schools, likely would handle the bulk of the distribution directly to students, and there could be a further partnership with school newspapers.

With such contributions from kids and schools holding down costs, there should be little question of whether such an enterprise could be self-sustaining or even profitable. Considerable sponsorship money is available for youth-oriented projects, but the entrepreneurial newspaper should be able to generate new advertising aimed at young people as a huge market segment. After all, teenagers were expected to spend $57 billion of their own money in 1992, 16 percent more than 1991, according to Teenage Research Unlimited, and younger kids will toss another $8.5 billion into the economy. Even if the profit is not there, a newspaper should consider the modest investment, not only for altruism but for its own future.

Inclusiveness

A market-driven newspaper must be representative of the people in the community. The 1990 census revealed volatile racial and ethnic changes. "In the field of population statistics, where change sometimes seems glacially slow, the speed at which the country's racial mix was altered in the 1980s was breathtaking," the *New York Times* reported. "The rate of increase in the minority population was nearly twice as fast as in the 1970s. And much of the surge was among those of Hispanic ancestry, an increase of 7.7 million people, or 53 percent, over 1980."[59] While the white population grew only 6 percent, African Americans increased 13 percent and Asian Americans 108 percent. There is an increasingly open and cohesive lesbian and gay community.

Newspapers remain overwhelmingly middle-class, college-educated, white, male institutions in their staffing, outlook, and coverage.

The industry has long been committed to achieving representative racial, gender, and ethnic diversity on newsroom staffs, and it has made significant progress, against great odds. But while they work toward proportional representation on their staffs, editors now must recognize the nation's churning demographics and achieve diversity within the content of the newspaper. We tend to cover "them" as phenomena or issues, as if they are removed from "our" mainstream. Until they are part of us, we must find innovative ways to make our newspaper theirs too.

It doesn't just happen; inertia is powerful. *USA Today* has taken the lead, simply by mandating that certain stories, pages, photos, and positions must include a minority and/or a woman—one of their editors called it "beating back the white guys." Other ideas are to include public members on the editorial board, develop representative columnists, methodically learn about all of a newspaper's communities, and institutionalize ways of talking with and listening to them. We need to routinize coverage of minority communities, day in and day out, and launch reporting projects inspired by their needs—not, for example, just the annual tribute to Crispus Attucks and Rosa Parks during Black History Month. In two remarkable national roundtables called "Demography and Democracy," New Directions for News developed some radical, but doable, ideas, such as a "democracy mall" to take a different kind of populist journalism into alienated communities.

As our society continues to discover that women and men indeed are different in more ways than physiological, it is worth speculating how newspapers edited predominantly by women might be different from those edited by men and by women conditioned to edit like men. Would news judgments still concentrate on conflict (wars and crime) and competition (spectator sports and political infighting)? Or might they discover more real-people news—as we call it in our newsroom, that is, news that touches people's lives—and seek more resolution of the issues of our society? Would we still cover school-board battles but not classroom education? Would we still have a reporter chasing salacious details of the juiciest crime but no one covering day care?

Credibility

Since 1985, when the ASNE Credibility Committee reported a dangerous credibility gap between newspapers and the public,[60] editors have come a long way in opening up to their readers. Editors listen more, they give readers the benefit of the doubt, they write columns explaining the paper, they publish their addresses and phone numbers, they ask for feedback and publish more of it.

But as the Kettering report shows, citizens still say they don't believe newspapers. They still tend to think they are part of some sort of game that smells like a conspiracy. Pat Buchanan, a wealthy columnist, runs for president, and John Sununu, former presidential chief of staff, replaces him at CNN. How does one tell them apart anymore? The public sees the spin doctors at work and having their way with grinning reporters. Political writers are courted by, then become pals with, those whom they cover. The Washington press corps is more a press clique, playing favorites in the silly game of horse-race politics. Readers are confused and angry about real issues—crime, disintegrating families, deteriorating schools, pollution, costly health care, fading values—and their journalists are throwing gridiron roasts for politicos and writing earnestly about whether George Bush likes broccoli and whether Bill Clinton cheated on his wife.

Part of journalists' problem may be that they have become overprofessionalized, with increasingly restrictive membership requirements. They have come to think of themselves as a privileged club, shielded by the first law of the land, the First Amendment. Freedom of the press, of course, was not meant to create a powerful, rich media elite. It was—is—intended to protect free and open communication and discussion of information and ideas among the citizenry. There is an argument that, as news media become bigger, richer, and more aloof, they are becoming more removed from the spirit of the First Amendment. Newspapers are not the First Amendment; they are potentially its most loyal and effective servant.

Newspaper journalists must decide whether they will be the people's journalists. If they so choose, then they must break with the privileges and the chumminess, step over to the side of the public and cover the world from their perspective, with their interests, anger, and frustration. When editors and reporters are arrogant, silly, superficial, and suspicious, people will find newspapers amusing enough to buy now and then, but over the long run, they will continue to find them dispensable. As was pointed out in *The New News v. The Old News: The Press and Politics in the 1990s*, the first volume in this series, it was often the public that asked presidential candidates the important questions, reminding journalists and talk show hosts that focusing on rumors and horse-race issues just wasn't enough.

Democratic Connection

Because television, except in the broadest way, has failed in its early potential as a facilitator of democracy, newspapers remain the last best hope of connecting citizens with their governance. As the Kettering research suggested and the 1992 presidential campaign illustrated, many "apathetic" Americans do want to participate in the democracy, if they feel their involvement matters. Given this public appetite, the democratic mission of newspapers—while driven by societal and constitutional responsibility—should find support in the marketplace.

This mission might comprise three strategies. The first, of course, is journalism, not only in the traditional monitoring and watchdog functions, but also by providing empowerment to citizens, particularly through explanation and help. Rather than the common incomprehensible stories rife with bureaucratese, jargon, and insider games, democratic journalism would be reported and written from the perspective of the citizen, explaining situations and processes and why she or he should care and providing tools for individual involvement. For just one example, on every city council story, could not the newspaper tell the reader specifically how to comment to the appropriate official?

The second strategy is on what traditionally has been considered the business side. Some newspaper companies shamelessly have used the First Amendment for purely economic ends, and it is time for them to fulfill the responsibility side of freedom of the press. A business strategy would go beyond the product to the other P's in the marketing mix—price, place, and promotion. Tiered pricing, as discussed above, could put the newspaper in more low-income homes. A distribution policy would make home delivery available everywhere within reasonable reach of a truck—without cutting off areas of low advertiser interest, low circulation penetration, or high crime. A promotion initiative could present the newspaper not just as good reading or a helpful friend but also as a tool of empowerment for the individual—maybe even as essential to fulfilling one's personal democratic responsibility.

The third strategy is leadership, both within the pages of the newspaper and in the community.

Leadership

The institutions that have held this society together for so long—the family, church, workplace, local and national power structures—have changed, some for the better, some not. Whatever one might think of the institutions individually, their collective diminution has created a vacuum of leadership that may be filled by the mindless cultural icon of television.

The cumulative impact of the above strategies for the new newspaper could be summed up in one grander strategy: leadership. Given the disintegration of society and the loss of faith in many of its institutions—particularly government—newspapers have an opportunity to reinvent the newspaper as the best hope for leading in ways great and small.

Jay Rosen, a journalism professor at New York University, says most newspapers assume the existence of a public "out there" interested and involved in public affairs. In fact, he argues, society has become so splintered that, before a newspaper can inform the public, it must form a public. In his essay "Politics, Vision, and the Press," and elsewhere, he cites the work of the Columbus (Georgia) *Ledger-Enquirer*, whose major reporting project on the future of the city was largely ignored until the paper itself took the lead in organizing citizen involvement. In a call for a "commitment to citizenship," Rosen says in one article:

> To be adversarial, critical, to ask the tough questions, to expose scandal and wrongdoing . . . these are necessary tasks, even noble tasks, but they are also negative tasks. Other than the vague injunction to "inform the public" we have yet to define the journalist's mission positively. We have yet to ask what journalists should be in favor of, particularly in the realm of politics. So I ask you: What are journalists in favor of, and what should they be in favor of, not as individuals with their own views but as professionals with a public mission? My preferred answer is that journalism, and specifically the newspaper, ought to become a support system for public life.[61]

The suggestion is not for newspapers to move their editorial page to the front page or otherwise abandon the independence of their news columns. It is that, rather than merely reacting to news that happens "out there," the newspaper take more responsibility—leadership—in laying out a public agenda and using its power affirmatively to see that the citizenry pays attention and that other institutions respond.

It is too easy for the public to avoid involvement and for government to avoid commitment. The new newspaper likely will be the only institution representing the people that can be strong and independent enough to identify the needs and weaknesses in our society, investigate them, and by using its best attempts at truth, mobilize the people to action. This will make a difference not only at the level of the big national newspapers but also, and perhaps particularly, at every local newspaper that claims to be one. The new newspaper will damn the power structures, sensitivities, traditions, and journalism contests and use its considerable and unique resources to attack the toughest problems of the people in its town. If people care about their communities and their democracy—and they do—the newspaper will be rewarded in the marketplace.

With such a rich array of attributes and opportunities, from the amusement of the crossword puzzle to the higher functions of a democratic free press, the daily newspaper can come to feel more twenty-first century than nineteenth. While it is difficult to see a future for those 20 and 30 percent profit margins, there can be a clear vision for a dynamic and profitable mix of advertising niches, diversification of news/advertising products, helpfulness, compelling and responsive news content, and community leadership. The value—the market value, if you will—of the daily newspaper perseveres at many levels of American life.

During summer 1992, the people of Pittsburgh experienced life without their newspapers. When the unions struck the *Pittsburgh Press* and *Pittsburgh Post-Gazette*, attendance at the division-leading Pirates baseball games fell, readers complained about the lack of news, couples worried about their wedding announcements, movie theaters and their patrons struggled to connect, job hunters didn't know where to look, friends unknowingly missed funerals, playgoers stayed home from what reviews would have called the best play of the season, real estate companies tried to advertise on television, and talk shows had nothing to talk about: Radio call-in host Bill Green said, "Things seemed very slow no matter what I would throw out there to discuss. Then it hit me: There's no local newspaper, so people can't relate to what I am saying or say, 'Did you read about that dumb thing the city council did?'"[62]

And worst, of course, the local government took advantage of the silence to pass a new $1 monthly tax on telephones. "I bet if the papers were publishing they would have at least taken a position," Green said. "It would have been a cause célèbre in this town."

If newspapers succeed in reinvigorating themselves to change with their readers, they will know, by the circulation numbers and journalism's value and power in society. If they fail, they will know when power settles on the elite, educated few, when reading becomes an envied ticket to the ruling class, and when a newspaper subscription becomes a status symbol.

Notes

1. Walt Potter, "Amid Uncertainty, Forecasters Look for Signs for Recovery," *Presstime*, January 1992, pp. 18–26.
2. Deborah J. MacInnis and Bernard Jaworski, "Information Processing from Advertisements: Toward an Integrative Framework," *Journal of Marketing* 53 (October 1989).
3. Leo Bogart, *Press and Public: Who Reads What, When, Where, and Why in American Newspapers*, 2nd ed. (Hillsdale, N.J.: Erlbaum, 1989), p. 144.
4. W. Russell Neuman, *The Paradox of Mass Politics: Knowledge and Opinion in the American Electorate* (Cambridge, Mass.: Harvard University Press, 1986).
5. "Citizens and Politics: A View from Main Street America," Report prepared for the Kettering Foundation by the Harwood Group, Dayton, Ohio, June 1991.
6. "Newspaper Credibility: Building Reader Trust," Report of the Credibility Committee, American Society of Newspaper Editors, Reston, Virginia, April 1985.
7. Marvin Kalb, "The Nixon Memo," Discussion Paper D-13, The Joan Shorenstein Barone Center, John F. Kennedy School of Government, Harvard University, July 1992.
8. Bogart, *Press and Public*, p. 144.
9. Ibid., p. 91.
10. Virginia Dodge Fielder and Beverly A. Barnum, "Love Us and Leave Us: New Subscribers One Year Later," Report of the Readership and Research Committee, American Society of Newspaper Editors, Reston, Virginia, April 1987.
11. Nancy Gibbs, "How America Has Run Out of Time," *Time*, April 24, 1989, pp. 58–67.
12. Gary Burtless, "Are We All Working Too Hard? It's Better Than Watching Oprah," *Wall Street Journal*, January 4, 1990, p. A14.
13. Juliet B. Schor, *The Overworked American: The Unexpected Decline of Leisure* (New York: Basic Books, 1991).
14. Christina Robb (*Boston Globe*), "Where Has Our Free Time Gone? Experts Say It's Squandered on Television," *Wisconsin State Journal*, March 1, 1992, p. D6. The major project in which Robinson participated is described in depth in F. Thomas Juster and Frank P. Stafford, eds., *Time, Goods, and Well-Being* (Ann Arbor: Survey Research Center, Institute for Social Research, University of Michigan, 1985).

15. Ken Sacharin, "Media Capitals: A Report on Americans' Media Use by Market," Young & Rubicam, San Francisco, 1992.

16. Allen C. Bluedorn (University of Missouri–Columbia), Carol Felker Kaufman (Rutgers University), and Paul M. Lane (Western Michigan University), "How Many Things Do You Like to Do at Once? An Introduction to Monochronic and Polychronic Time," Unpublished manuscript, February 7, 1992. Carol Felker Kaufman, Paul M. Lane, and Jay D. Lindquist, "Exploring More Than 24 Hours a Day: A Preliminary Investigation of Polychronic Time Use," *Journal of Consumer Research* 18 (December 1991): 392–401.

17. Carol Hymowitz, "Trading Fat Paychecks for Free Time," *Wall Street Journal*, August 5, 1991, p. B1.

18. Irwin S. Kirsch and Ann Jungeblut, *Literacy: Final Report;* also *Literacy: Profiles of America's Young Adults* (Princeton, N.J.: National Assessment of Educational Progress, Educational Testing Service, 1986).

19. Georgia M. Green, "Organization, Goals and Comprehensibility in Narratives: Newswriting, a Case Study," Technical Report No. 132, Center for the Study of Reading, University of Illinois at Urbana-Champaign, 1979.

20. Ibid., p. 45.

21. E. D. Hirsch, Jr., *Cultural Literacy: What Every American Needs to Know* (Boston: Houghton Mifflin, 1987).

22. James Trefil, "Science Matters in Changing Society," *Wisconsin State Journal*, November 24, 1991. A commentary on his book *Science Matters: Achieving Scientific Literacy* (New York: Doubleday, 1990).

23. "A National Survey of American Economic Literacy," a report by the National Center for Research in Economic Education at the University of Nebraska and the Gallup Organization for the National Council on Economic Education, 1992 (Princeton, N.J.: Gallup Organization Education Research Division, 1992).

24. Mitchell Stephens, "The Death of Reading: Will a Nation That Stops Reading Eventually Stop Thinking?" *Los Angeles Times Magazine*, September 22, 1991, pp. 10–16, 42–44.

25. "Facts about Newspapers," American Newspaper Publishers Association, 1991.

26. Stephens, p. 12.

27. Albert E. Gollin, "Setting the Record Straight on Trends in Newspaper Readership," *Presstime*, April 1992, p. 42.

28. "Facts about Newspapers"; Nancy M. Davis, "Fight for Your Slice," *Presstime*, August 1992, p. 22.

29. Neil Postman, *Amusing Ourselves to Death: Public Discourse in the Age of Show Business* (New York: Viking Penguin, 1985).

30. Ibid., p. 50.

31. Sound bite averages are for network news coverage only, not including CNN. Figures come from the Democracy '92 Project, headed by professors Marion Just and Ann Crigler for the Joan Shorenstein Barone Center, Harvard University.

32. Postman, *Amusing Ourselves to Death*, pp. 87, 90.

33. Postman, *Amusing Ourselves to Death*, pp. 60, 61.

34. Robert MacNeil, "Is Television Decreasing Our Attention Span?" *New York University Education Quarterly* 14, no. 2 (Winter 1983) 2.

35. Postman, *Amusing Ourselves to Death*, p. 7, 22, 24, 27, 31, 110–11.

36. Jane M. Healy, *Endangered Minds: Why Our Children Don't Think* (New York: Simon & Schuster, 1990).

37. Ibid., pp. 199–200.

38. "America's Smallest School: The Family" (Princeton, N.J.: Educational Testing Service, 1992).

39. John P. Robinson and Mark R. Levy, *The Main Source: Learning from Television News* (Beverly Hills, Calif.: Sage, 1986).

40. John Morton, "Where Have All the Readers Gone?" *Washington Journalism Review*, April 1992, p. 56.

41. Deborah Walker and Jane Wilson, "The Battle for Waterloo," a Supplement to *Presstime*, September 1991.

42. William B. Blankenburg, "The Viability of the Comprehensive Daily Newspaper," Paper presented at the Association for Education in Journalism and Mass Communication Convention, Montreal, August 6, 1992.

43. Ibid., p. 7.

44. For example: Bogart, *Press and Public*, pp. 343–44; Stephen Lacy, "The Financial Commitment Approach to News Media Competition," *Journal of Media Economics*, Summer 1992, pp. 5–21; William B. Blankenburg and Robert L. Friend, "The Effects of Cost and Revenue Strategies on Circulation," Paper presented to the Newspaper Research Council Spring Conference, Orlando, Florida, April 13, 1992.

45. John Markoff, "A Media Pioneer's Quest: Portable Electronic Newspapers," *New York Times*, June 28, 1992, p. 11.

46. Stephens, p. 44.

47. Warren Buffett, "A Change in Media Economics and Some Valuation Mass," Letter to shareholders, Berkshire Hathaway annual report, 1991.

48. Blankenburg and Friend, "Effects of Cost and Revenue Strategies."

49. Bogart, *Press and Public*, p. 343. The Newspaper Readership Project is discussed in depth in Leo Bogart, *Preserving the Press: How Daily Newspapers Mobilized to Keep Their Readers* (New York: Columbia University Press, 1991).

50. Peter T. Kilborn, "Paperboys and Papergirls Turn a Last Corner," *New York Times*, August 16, 1992, p. 14.

51. Bogart, *Press and Public*, is the best single collection of published newspaper research.

52. Sonia M. Livingstone, "The Resourceful Reader: Interpreting Television Characters and Narratives," *Communication Yearbook*, forthcoming.

53. Felicia Pratto and Oliver P. John, "Automatic Vigilance: The Attention-Grabbing Power of Negative Social Information," *Journal of Personality and Social Psychology* 61, no. 3 (1991).

54. William Paisley, "Communication Research as a Behavioral Discipline," Unpublished paper, Institute for Communication Research, Stanford University, 1969.

55. Joan Meyers-Levy and Durairaj Maheswaran, "Exploring Differences in Males' and Females' Processing Strategies," *Journal of Consumer Research* 18 (June 1991).

56. Richard Saul Wurman, *Information Anxiety* (New York: Doubleday, 1989).

57. Albert E. Gollin, "An Assessment of Trends in U.S. Newspaper Circulation and Readership," Newspaper Advertising Bureau, New York, December 1991.

58. "Keys to Our Survival," Report of the Readership and Research and Future of Newspapers committees, American Society of Newspaper Editors, Reston, Virginia, April 1991.

59. Felicity Barringer, "Census Shows Profound Change in Racial Makeup of the Nation," *New York Times,* March 11, 1991, p. A1.

60. "Newspaper Credibility."

61. Jay Rosen, "Forming and Informing the Public," Kettering Review, Winter 1992, pp. 69–70.

62. Pat Guy, "Strikes Leaves Pittsburgh in the Dark," *USA Today,* July 29, 1992.

Yesterday's News:
Why Newspapers Are
Losing Their Franchise

by Howard Kurtz

An Endangered Species

The newspaper business is still reeling from its worst downturn since the Great Depression. Papers across the country, from the most prestigious to the most pedestrian, have been laying off employees and closing bureaus. The proportion of households reading a daily newspaper continues to shrink, as it has for the past thirty years. More than 150 papers have folded since 1970.

Newspapers are losing ground—to television networks such as Cable News Network (CNN) and C-SPAN, direct mail, home computers and fax machines, niche magazines, home shopping clubs, books-on-tape, and a hundred other leisure pursuits. The prototypical newspaper movie is no longer *All the President's Men*, the story of how Bob Woodward and Carl Bernstein cracked the Watergate scandal, but *Absence of Malice*, a dark tale in which reporter Sally Field libels businessman Paul Newman. The quintessential television series is no longer "Lou Grant," the hard-bitten city editor, but "Murphy Brown," featuring simpletons like Frank Fontana and Corky Sherwood.

Big chains have gobbled up dozens of independent dailies, turning them into assembly-line products with lots of short stories, colorful charts, and full-page weather maps. There is a deep-rooted fear, even at the biggest papers, that much of the audience has tuned out, leaving us writing for a small, self-important elite. Noisy, dirty printing presses seem ancient in an era of satellite communications. We are becoming an endangered species.

In the face of this debilitating decline, most of the nation's 1,580 daily newspapers are desperately trying to reinvent themselves. But some of these changes are taking the industry in precisely the wrong direction, while others do not go nearly far enough. Tinkering and half-measures will no longer do the trick.

The slow decline of the newspaper business masks a basic paradox. Most newspapers in the 1990s are better written and better edited than those at any other time in history. The journalists who produce them are better educated and more specialized, in fields ranging from medicine to foreign policy to computer technology, than their predecessors. The profession's ethical standards, once something of a joke, have never been higher. The work force, whose doors were long closed to minorities and women, has never been more diverse. And never before have publishers and editors struggled so mightily to divine the desires of their readers—or "customers," in the current catchphrase—and to deliver the goods. And yet somehow these efforts continue to fall short.

This report will examine the underlying reasons for the industry's malaise, which has been gathering force since the 1970s. Four case studies—involving *USA Today*, the Boca Raton *News*, the *Arkansas Gazette*, and the *New York Times*—will examine how different newspapers with very different missions have tried, with mixed success, to attract new readers and turn occasional readers into steady customers. I will also offer my prescriptions for how newspapers can regain their edge and vitality in an era dominated by television.

A brief look at the demographic trends affecting the newspaper business suggests that there is indeed cause for alarm. In 1967, 73 percent of American adults said they read a newspaper every day. By 1991 that figure had dropped to just 51 percent. Daily newspaper circulation has hovered around sixty-two million for the past twenty-five years, even as the country's adult population grew by more than a third.

Put another way, where 132 newspapers were sold for each hundred American households in 1930, by 1986 the figure had dropped to 72. A more detailed analysis shows that the core newspaper audience is older, more affluent, and better educated than nonreaders. This trend could find newspapers confined to an aging socioeconomic elite, while most of the country receives its news and information elsewhere. More than 60 percent of college graduates say they read a newspaper every day, compared to less than half of those with a high school education or less. More than 60 percent of those in the top quarter of the income scale are daily readers, compared to less than 40 percent of those in the bottom quarter. (Even among college graduates, daily readership has dropped off by 20 percent since 1972.)

Age (or, from another perspective, generation) is another crucial factor. More than 70 percent of those over sixty years old are daily readers, compared to less than 30 percent of those aged eighteen to twenty-nine. And a noticeable gender gap has developed among those under age thirty-five, with 7 to 9 percent fewer women than men describing themselves as regular newspaper readers.

In every category, the trend lines are headed south. In the early 1970s, just under half of people aged eighteen to twenty-nine read a paper each day, compared to about a quarter now. For those with less than a high school education, daily readership dropped from 60 percent to about 45 percent. In the lowest quarter of the income scale, the rate has dipped from 55 percent to under 40 percent. There has been similar slippage among the most loyal demographic groups, except for those over age sixty.

The notion that younger people have simply stopped reading is something of a myth. Library circulation of juvenile books increased 33 percent from 1980 to 1987. Sales of juvenile books jumped 250 percent from 1972 to 1986. People in their teens and twenties comprise a major portion of the readership of such magazines as *Rolling Stone*, *Mademoiselle*, and *GQ*. They are simply less interested in what newspapers have to offer.[1]

Still, many remain occasional readers. For example, 81 percent of teenagers (ages twelve to seventeen), the least interested age group, say they read a newspaper at least once a week. Younger people might be drawn to the weekend entertainment section or the Sunday sports section, but they are not motivated to pick up the paper during the week. The industry's challenge is to find the formula that will transform these occasional readers into steady customers.

In the past, even occasional newspaper readers often became steady customers by their mid- to late twenties, when they were more likely to own a home and put down roots in a community. But studies show that those who never bothered with newspapers when they were growing up are least likely to acquire the habit in middle age. In short, if editors don't find a way to hook the younger generation, they can kiss the future good-bye.

I have been thinking about these problems since the mid-1970s, most recently as the media reporter for the *Washington Post*. I have seen the business evolve from manual typewriters and dreary black-and-white layouts to the age of computer graphics, color weather maps, and special sections aimed at everyone from teenagers to sports nuts. After more than a decade in various reporting jobs at the *Post*, and before that at the now-deceased *Washington Star* and the *Record* in Bergen County, New Jersey, I have lived through endless waves of redesigns, reshufflings, and planning meetings, all meant to improve the packaging, and sometimes the substance, of daily journalism.

Clearly, the industry is at a crossroads. Dozens of papers are now following the path pioneered by *USA Today*, a tighter-and-brighter philosophy designed to cater to the short attention span of the video generation.

The problem is that the cure may be worse than the disease. The cumulative effect of these changes is to deemphasize news and replace it with a feel-good product that is more frivolous, less demanding, more like television. And television already does it better.

The salvation of daily journalism, in my view, lies in those qualities that separate us from television: depth, texture, analysis, and intensive and sophisticated reporting. There is some historical evidence for the assertion that high-quality papers prosper over the long run. The *New York Times* increased its news coverage during World War II, while other papers were emphasizing advertising, and gained a loyal readership that cemented its place atop the elite New York market. The *Washington Post* came to dominate its circulation area after embarking on an expansion in the late 1960s that eventually doubled the size of the staff. Knight-Ridder, long one of the more enlightened newspaper groups, spent considerable sums in the 1970s and early 1980s to improve the *Philadelphia Inquirer*, now a prosperous paper that has outlasted its competition. *USA Today*, meanwhile, has yet to turn a profit ten years after it was started.

During the Persian Gulf War, most Americans were glued to their television sets to try to keep up with the fast-moving events. With CNN providing live coverage of each Scud missile attack, some prognosticators declared newspapers obsolete. But newspaper circulation rose during the war, by hundreds of thousands of copies in some cases, because people needed print reporters to help them sort out the jumble of disconnected images. Once their appetite for news had been whetted, they wanted more. (Of course, it wasn't until months after the war that reporters for *Newsday*, the *Army Times*, and the *Washington Post* revealed how the military withheld information on deaths caused by "friendly fire," the lower success rate of American bombs, and other inconvenient details the Pentagon had failed to release. But newspapers broke the story, not television.)

Newspapers are also better positioned than the behemoths of broadcasting to provide the kind of localized coverage that readers increasingly demand. The expansion of cable television has produced more stations devoted to local news, but even these stations must appeal to viewers across a broad metropolitan area with numerous political jurisdictions. For someone interested in finding out about property taxes or neighborhood crime, the plan for a new town library or a textbook shortage at the local junior high, television is simply too broad gauged an instrument that, as Frank Denton points out in his paper, often ignores stories that are not visual. Newspapers are uniquely positioned to provide the fine print, the sharper focus. Some of the nation's best papers—including the *Los Angeles Times* (daily circulation 1.3 million), *Chicago Tribune* (723,000), *St. Petersburg Times* (361,000), and *Hartford Courant* (235,000)—are increasingly using zoned editions to make local news the linchpin of their franchise.

There are some hopeful signs that serious journalism is making a comeback. In the fall of 1991, Donald L. Barlett and James B. Steele of the *Philadelphia Inquirer* provided a classic example of the power of newspaper reporting. The Pulitzer Prize-winning team struck a nerve with their nine-part series on "how the game was rigged against the middle class" by Washington rulemakers and corporate power brokers. Based on two years of research and interviews in fifty cities, stories ranged from how a factory relocation eliminated the job of a woman earning $7.91 an hour to a 2,184 percent increase in millionaires' salaries during the 1980s.[2] Each piece ran at least three full pages, far outstripping the supposed attention span of today's readers. Yet security guards had to be summoned to quiet crowds who came to the lobby demanding reprints. The *Inquirer* eventually distributed 400,000 reprints and received 20,000 letters, and the series was expanded into a best-selling book.

For much of the industry, however, the trend is in precisely the opposite direction. Everyone wants to be "reader-friendly," the buzzword of the 1990s. Hard news is out; relevance is in. Hundreds of papers have undergone virtually identical redesigns, with colorful indexes and pictures and little boxes above the logo touting fun stories inside. "Let's Go Barefoot!" says the "skybox" atop the *Charlotte Observer* logo, with a cartoon picture of two feet. "Jammin' Jamaica— It's Reggae Time," says the *Miami Herald*'s skybox. "A Star Trek Quiz," says the *Hartford Courant*'s box. There are car columns, health columns, gossip columns, advice columns, lawyers' columns, computer columns, photography columns, gardening columns, men's columns, women's columns, fishing columns, finance columns. There are parenting tips, survival tips, pet tips, dining tips, shopping tips, travel tips. There are sections called "You," "Sunday Brunch," "Almost the Weekend," "High Style," "Home," "View," "Scene," "Tempo," "Living," "Life," "Yo," and "Yo! Info!"

There's nothing wrong with most of these features, whether it is a look at the problems of two-career couples, a guide to area sushi bars, another profile of Warren Beatty, or pointers on the perfect dinner party. Newspapers are meant to be smorgasbords, and some people will always buy them for the television listings or the grocery coupons. Nor is there any harm in loosening our ties and shedding some of our stuffiness. But at too many newspapers the trendy stuff has all but replaced a commitment to news.

Few editors will admit this, of course. Most proclaim their undying commitment to informing the public, even as some reduce national news to half a page and foreign news to a few wire-service briefs. But many of them are devoting a growing share of their budgets to fuzzy feature sections that also happen to be magnets for advertising. Too many editors have become focus-group groupies, determined to offer citizens no more than what they say they want. Readers don't like stories that jump to another page? They don't want boring news about government? They don't care about Africa and Asia? Fine! Let's add a wine column and have more stories about jogging.

Newsrooms are filled with what Kurt Luedtke, a screenwriter and former executive editor of the *Detroit Free Press*, calls "marketing talk." "How about the kids? Let's put younger stuff in the paper! How about old folks? How come they're not reading the paper? If they want a coin column, we'll give them a coin column. If they want a horoscope, we'll give them a horoscope. You wind up with this horrible, pallid, bland mishmash."

The new emphasis is on service pieces aimed at upscale baby boomers with lots of disposable income. Many editors are boomers, after all, and many yuppies live in the suburbs, where newspapers have been redoubling their efforts. Left out of the equation are poor people, blue-collar workers, and minorities, but advertisers are less interested in them anyway. Coverage of minorities is better than a generation ago—in part because newspapers have belatedly begun to diversify their staffs—but marketing is another story. The *Nashville Tennessean*, for example, simply doesn't deliver to some ghetto neighborhoods or place newspaper racks there. Many of the afternoon papers and tabloids that once appealed to the lunch-bucket crowd, from the *Chicago Daily News* to the *Philadelphia Bulletin*, are now defunct, and their readers have defected in droves to television and specialized magazines.

"Look at the front page," says Mike Barnicle, a columnist for the metropolitan section of the *Boston Globe*. "More often than not it's full of what I call made-up stories, ideas they cook up at these . . . meetings: 'Go out and do left-handed teenagers who are thinking of becoming gay.' They do trends. They don't do news. The only time they do news is when a hurricane comes, and that they can plan for.

Four out of seven days you will not find the word 'yesterday' on the metro page.

"There are many, many editors who . . . don't have a clue as to what might interest a reader. There's a burnt fuse, a lack of connection between people in the business and a large number of people who read newspapers."

Our efforts to repair this burnt fuse are sometimes laughable. We hire teenagers to review movies for other teens and feel like we've suddenly plugged into the youth culture. We assign reporters to cover shopping malls. We ballyhoo the local football team on the front page. We shy away from what J. Keith Moyer, editor of Gannett's Rochester *Democrat & Chronicle* and the *Times-Union*, calls "spinach journalism," as in "Eat this, it's good for you."

Some owners make no bones about this approach. John C. Gardner, former publisher of the *Quad-City Times* in Davenport, Iowa (circulation 55,000), and now president of the Quad-City Development Group, says he relied heavily on readership surveys to "tailor our product to the market. Our readers tell us, 'We don't want to work terribly hard, we don't want to struggle through what you're trying to tell us.' They like stories they can use for their coffee-break talk."[3]

The problem is that too often we're talking down to people, and they know it. Instead of capturing their attention the hard way—with well-reported, well-written stories about schools and taxes and crime and culture and other things that matter in their lives—we tend to take the easy way out and feed them cotton candy.

Critics will suggest that my prescription for more in-depth journalism flies in the face of economic reality. Obviously, the first responsibility of any publisher is to keep the ship afloat; we don't need any more dead newspapers sacrificed on the altar of high-minded journalism. Admittedly, my proposal is hardly a quick fix; instead, it presumes that strong and substantive newspapers prosper over the long haul, and that an investment in better reporting now will produce more loyal readers down the road.

The fact is, people will read: On the one day when they have time to read and relax, newspapers have become a fixture in more and more homes. Sunday circulation, the one bright spot in newspaper sales, jumped 26 percent, from forty-nine million in 1970 to sixty-two million in 1988. Sunday is the day when newspapers are most like magazines—with well-crafted features, special sections, provocative opinion pieces—and least dependent on incremental government news.

To be sure, a newspaper's profitability rests on a variety of factors, some of which have little to do with the quality of its reporting. First and foremost is the state of the economy. Lots of bad newspapers made plenty of money in the 1980s, and plenty of good ones have seen their profits plummet during the early 1990s. In some cities, the shrinkage of the retail market has badly eroded the advertising base, while declining housing prices and a languishing real estate market have taken a large bite out of classified ads. Labor costs, too, are crucial. The New York *Daily News*, with a one million-plus circulation, earned $4 billion in revenue during the 1980s, yet managed to lose $115 million. Thanks in part to inflated union contracts that required fourteen men on a press, or twice as many as the *News* needed, the paper simply cost too much to produce, and that helped push it into Chapter 11 bankruptcy, from which it only recently emerged.

Total daily circulation of newspapers in the United States declined from 62.3 million in 1990 to 60.7 million in 1991. Much of this had to do with the recession. There is also a strong correlation between circulation and newsstand price. Papers that have raised their prices from 25 to 35 or 50 cents in the past two years have invariably watched their sales decline, no matter how exciting their front pages might be.

Finally, even what we describe as "monopoly" newspapers face many sources of competition. As Jean Gaddy Wilson, head of an industry group called New Dimensions for News, has observed, newspapers now must vie with 12,000 magazines and newsletters, 8,500 weeklies, 350 commercial television stations, 500 public service television stations, 10,684 cable television systems, 9,500 radio stations, and 2,650 data-base services.[4] New technology, such as interactive television and telephone lines that carry classified advertising, promise to erode the revenue base still further. These are all valuable consumer services, but they make it that much harder for newspapers to turn a profit.

What follows, then, is not a sure-fire formula for profitability, but neither does it ignore marketplace realities. The plain fact is, in a world with dozens of sources of instantaneous information, there is no reason for people to buy newspapers unless they provide detailed, compelling material that can't be found elsewhere. And that means more than eight-inch stories and computer-generated charts. It means a willingness to tackle controversial subjects that have all but vanished from parts of the newspaper landscape.

The Problem with Newspapers

Newspapers are afflicted with what I call "creeping incrementalism." We take a handful of stories and chew them over and over, with second-day stories and third-day stories and ninth-day stories, until they are utterly devoid of flavor. We seize on minute developments and imbue them with cosmic significance: "House Clears Way for Vote on Rights Bill"; "Baker Urges Israeli Response on Talks"; "Economists at Odds on Recession"; "Bush Administration Ponders Response." We chronicle bureaucratic battles, deluding ourselves into believing that most people are as fascinated by the inner workings of government and politics as we are. We relentlessly round up experts who are as likely to be wrong as your dim-witted neighbor down the street. We tell you what happened yesterday when you've already seen it on the tube. No wonder people are turned off.

Newspapers have also entered an era of uniformity. As you travel around the country, it's hard to tell where you are by reading many local papers. They carry the same wire stories, the same syndicated columns. When there were three or four newspapers serving each market, they had distinct personalities—eccentric or irascible, crusading or corny. Now most of them look like they're put out by the same faceless market research folks.

Once you get beyond the dozen or so top markets, there are hundreds of breathtakingly mediocre newspapers out there. Most are uncontested monopolies, with no smaller paper nipping at their heels. The growth of chains such as Gannett, Knight-Ridder, and Thomson has stamped hundreds of one-newspaper towns with a certain ethos—what veteran Baltimore *Sun* political columnist Jack W. Germond calls "corporate journalism"—not quite awful, but awfully boring.

"So much of what we do in a newspaper just doesn't have any excitement," says Christian Anderson, associate publisher of the Orange County *Register* (circulation 348,000) in California. "What is there in newspapers today that has the passion that MTV has? Nothing."[5]

Kurt Luedtke, the former *Free Press* editor, says that "many, many people are figuring out they can get along without newspapers just fine. You look at most of them and say, 'Why in God's name am I supposed to read this thing?'"

"Send a kid to city hall and he will bring back two or three things that look and feel like news and we will put it in the paper," he says. "People have stopped reading the stuff. Look at the lead story on any local page and 92 percent of the time it's whatever the city council did today and it's duller than hell."

Author William Greider, who now writes for *Rolling Stone*, says he tried to challenge the conventional, what-happened-yesterday approach when he was a senior editor at the *Washington Post* in the early 1980s. "I would ask, 'Why the hell are we playing these stories at the top of the front page when they're all going to be on television tonight?' That argument just got blown out of the room with a harrumph and a groan."

To spice up the daily stew, editors are serving up a broad menu of life-style features—coping with problems from divorce to bedwetting, to the lowdown on dating services, to where to buy the best shiitake mushrooms. Packaging takes precedence over substance. Serious enterprise reporting, the kind that penetrates closed institutions and illuminates difficult subjects, is in short supply. It is costly, time-consuming, and much harder to pull off than a trend story about diets. Sometimes, after much time and money has been expended, the story doesn't pan out. Hard-hitting stories can also be risky for profit-minded publishers in an era of big libel awards.

Too many editors bend over backward these days to avoid controversy, particularly on the supercharged subjects of race, abortion, and homosexuality. In an age when almost any comment is offensive to some interest group, newspapers have modulated their voices to avoid alienating their audience. The result is a journalistic blandness that passively records both sides of the issues without coming to grips with what people are really thinking and saying.

For two decades, even as newspapers steadily lost market share, they continued to produce the equivalent of huge, gas-guzzling sedans with tail fins. They were bulky products, poorly designed, poorly printed, and poorly edited. Someone once calculated that it would take eighteen years for the average, thirty-minute-a-day reader to consume one year's output of the *Washington Post*. While wave after wave of Japanese imports finally convinced Detroit to change its wasteful ways, the newspaper business found itself ambushed by a domestic information explosion. City dwellers were fleeing to the suburbs and taking their advertising dollars with them. The metropolitan newspaper, for all its improvements, seemed about as nimble as a dinosaur.

"The nature of the population and the country have changed," says Ben Bagdikian, former dean of the graduate school of journalism at the University of California at Berkeley. "The public is better educated. They have more alternatives. The demands on newspapers are greater in a much more complicated world."

The old, reporter-driven newspaper of the 1970s, with its interminable series on nuclear energy or solid waste that no one but a Pulitzer board could love, paid scant attention to the reader. The new method, as perfected by *USA Today*, is to meld multiple dispatches into one tight story, imparting to readers the maximum information in the shortest possible space. But while this approach may be economical, something vital—color, texture, nuance—is lost. Prose is mulched, compressed, and recycled to fit the format. Such a system makes desk-bound editors the supreme architects of the daily product, reducing reporters to fact-gathering drones.

Perhaps it is no coincidence that many newsrooms have taken on an insurance company atmosphere, with serious young people churning out serious stories as if they were legal briefs on product liability. Newspaper staffs are obviously better educated than two decades ago, and more practitioners are journalism school graduates or have earned other advanced degrees. The staffs are more racially diverse as well, thanks to fifteen years of affirmative action programs. But the overall outlook, for better or worse, is firmly rooted in upper-middle-class values. The oddballs, louts, and curmudgeons of yesteryear are a dwindling presence.

"There's no tolerance for people who get a little older or drink a little too much at lunch," says Phil Gailey, editorial page editor of the *St. Petersburg Times* and a veteran of Knight-Ridder, the *Washington Star*, and the *New York Times*. "These days most journalists are interested in getting on TV or writing books or both. The soul has gone out of the business."

Today's reporters, says Richard Cohen, an acerbic national columnist for the *Washington Post*, "are better educated and talented, but they ain't got no style. They don't know how to write a column from a bar, and they don't know how to write a column from a charity ball. They are boring, middle-class, technocratically-oriented people. I'm not seeing any writing that stands out, where you could take the byline off and I'd know it's them. There's no voice."

A Brief History

Few marketing tricks are available today that were not trotted out 160 years ago by James Gordon Bennett, the twice-failed publisher who launched the *New York Herald*. In 1835, when respectable newspapers were selling for 6 cents, his was one of the first penny papers. Newsboys hawked them on the streets. Bennett introduced lively prose and expanded Wall Street coverage. He played up lurid crimes, such as a murder at "one of the most splendid establishments devoted to infamous intercourse." He opened a Washington bureau. He assembled a network of correspondents in European capitals—the first time any American paper had done so—and sent boats to retrieve their dispatches from incoming ships. Rivals were forced to make their papers more readable and up to date.[6]

Bennett was not a stickler for propriety. He accepted licentious ads for a "personals" column and sold space to hawkers of quack medicines. In later years he would run serialized romances on the front page. An 1840 boycott by readers and advertisers, accusing the *Herald* of "reckless depravity," cut into his circulation, but not for long. The penny-paper phenomenon spread to Boston, Philadelphia, Baltimore, and other urban centers.

Technology gave the industry a major boost. By the 1840s the steam-driven press, ten times faster than the best hand press, dominated the American market. The telegraph became a journalistic fixture after the Baltimore *Sun* opened the first telegraph line between Washington and Baltimore. The penny papers used the new equipment during the 1846 war with Mexico, when timely dispatches were at a premium. The Associated Press, a cooperative that provided its members with national and foreign news, was born in 1848.

Most papers were openly partisan, a pattern that would change little for the next half-century. Horace Greeley, owner of the *New York Tribune*, was elected as a Whig member of Congress in 1848 and filed daily reports about waste and corruption in that institution.

Newspapers were never more vital than during the Civil War, when correspondents would race back with their bloody tales by train or horseback, sometimes providing first-hand accounts to President Lincoln. By the end of the 1860s the number of American newspapers was twice what it had been when the penny press began in 1833.

Professional qualifications soon began to rise. Charles Dana, editor of the *New York Sun*, favored college graduates for his staff in the 1880s. Reporters began receiving individual acclaim for the first time. Nellie Bly went around the world in eighty days, a publicity coup for Joseph Pulitzer's *New York World*. Henry Morton Stanley found Dr. Livingstone in Africa. Jacob Riis chronicled the ills of New York's "other half" for the *Tribune*. Richard Harding Davis of the *New York Journal* became the nation's most famous war correspondent.

Davis was a casualty of the sensational battles between Pulitzer's *World* and William Randolph Hearst's *Journal*, a forerunner of the great tabloid wars to come. In 1897, the *Journal* incited passions with a hyped-up Davis dispatch claiming that Spanish police had stripsearched women on an American ship bound for Key West. When the *World* exposed the story as overblown, Davis had to resign.

The media moguls of that era demanded drama. As Hearst cabled an artist he had dispatched to Cuba after the man complained that things were too quiet: "You furnish the pictures and I'll furnish the war." The yellow streak permeating journalism at the turn of the century left a vacuum for a more authoritative publication. Adolph Ochs, the publisher of the successful *Chattanooga Times,* bought the failing *New York Times* in 1896, when its circulation was a mere 9,000, compared to 600,000 for the *World* and 430,000 for the *Journal.* The *Times* huffed about journalistic standards and promoted itself as a newspaper that "does not soil the breakfast cloth." It offered complete financial coverage, bought better newsprint, and started a Saturday book review and illustrated Sunday supplement. But the breakthrough came from a marketing maneuver: Ochs lowered the price from 3 cents to a penny. Circulation quickly rose to 75,000 and by 1920 it reached 343,000.

Pulitzer's paper crusaded against such corporate giants as Standard Oil and the New York Central Railroad and exposed squalid conditions at Ellis Island. Lincoln Steffens, Ida Tarbell, and others became known as muckrakers, a term coined by Teddy Roosevelt. Self-promotion remained vital, even at the august *Times.* When the first transatlantic press cable was sent to the *Times* in 1907, the paper ran the Western Union message on page one with the accompanying headline: "Marconi Congratulates the *New York Times.*"

In what would seem an outrageous display of checkbook journalism today, the *Times* paid Admiral Robert Peary $4,000 for exclusive rights to the tale of his 1909 expedition to the North Pole. It did the same thing in 1927, signing Charles Lindbergh to a $5,000 contract (he eventually got $60,000) for the story of his pioneering flight to Paris. "When next heard from, Lindbergh will write the story of a great exploit for the readers of the *New York Times* and associated newspapers," Ochs's paper boasted in a front-page box.

Newspapers seemed to run out of gas during the 1930s, when money was tight, payrolls trimmed, and radio news on the ascent. In fact, newspapers were so worried about their new competitor that for a time they refused to carry radio listings. (The parallel to the recent evolution of cable television, which also delivers headlines round the clock, is inescapable, as is the renewed need for print journalism to provide what television, for all its immediacy, cannot.) The rise of Hitler shook the newspaper business out of its lethargy by feeding American hunger for foreign news. During the boom years of World War II, when many newspapers crammed their pages with advertising, the *Times* eschewed short-term profits and maintained the scope of its coverage. That helped cement the loyalty of its readership as other papers fell by the wayside, a lesson the struggling publishers of the 1990s would do well to remember.

The press's role as outside critic began to bloom during the civil rights strife of the early 1960s and achieved its full flowering during the Vietnam War. Most editorial pages initially backed the war, but that support crumbled under the weight of dispatches from correspondents like David Halberstam, Neil Sheehan, and Peter Arnett. Still, Vietnam was the first American conflict in which newspapers were no longer the principal means of communication. Television reporting came of age in the steamy jungles of that senseless war, achieving a dominance that would haunt the print side of the business for the next thirty years.

The 1960s were also a time when writers began their flirtation with the New Journalism, an impressionistic art form that was well suited to the cultural upheaval across the land. There was a sense that the old ways of defining news had failed to capture the anger and alienation in society, the changes in people's lives. It was, despite occasional excesses, a welcome transformation whose elements we now take for granted: that newspaper writing must be literate, entertaining, and allow for individual voices.

New Journalism was exemplified by the *New York Herald Tribune.* There was Jimmy Breslin spinning Runyonesque fables from the dark saloons of his native Queens; Tom Wolfe's impressionistic portraits of the more refined precincts of Manhattan; Art Buchwald's satiric pieces; Rowland Evans and Robert Novak's inside dope from the capital; Gail Sheehy's social trend-watching; Clay Felker editing the savvy Sunday supplement that would later become *New York* magazine.

The *Tribune's* death in 1966 was due largely to management's failure to win concessions from the city's powerful press unions. It was another reminder that inefficient, featherbedded newspapers, no matter how well written, cannot survive in the modern era. The *Tribune* was hardly alone. In 1900, New York City boasted twenty-five daily newspapers; by 1966 it was down to six, and a year later it was three.

Watergate proved the high-water mark of newspaper influence. Investigative reporting became a fixture of daily journalism in the 1970s, and even small papers started kicking over rocks in their municipal backyards. Millions of documents were suddenly available—under the Freedom of Information Act and campaign disclosure laws—and no public official or corporation was immune from scrutiny. Glorified by Hollywood, the press embarked on a new era of self-righteous muckraking as more reporters adopted an adversarial stance against government, determined to find fame and fortune by exposing official wrongdoing.

But the product still looked awful—gray, ink-smudged sheets with muddy pictures and dreary layouts. The 1980s were the decade of color, when packaging became paramount, when editors everywhere followed the lead of *USA Today*. It was also the decade when newspapers became huge money-makers.

The economics of the newspaper business changed forever when Wall Street got involved. As the big newspaper companies started going public—Times Mirror in 1964, Gannett in 1967, the New York Times Company in 1968, the Washington Post Company in 1971—they had to worry for the first time about shareholders and dividends and quarterly profits. Professional managers with an eye for the bottom line, like Walter Mattson, president of the New York Times Company, were bent on modernization and expansion, buying up other papers, magazines, paper mills, and fledgling cable franchises.

Allen Neuharth, the charismatic chairman of Gannett, mounted a propaganda campaign to change the industry's image on Wall Street in the 1960s and 1970s. His pitch was simple: Most of Gannett's papers were in small and medium-sized markets. They had little or no competition. They had no unions. They were lean, well-managed operations. It was the kind of appeal that many other newspaper executives would make in later years.

"We soon learned the Wall Street types were not interested in how many Pulitzer Prizes Gannett had won (a lot), or how good our editors and reporters were (very), or about our personal lifestyles," Neuharth says. "They wanted to know: What made Gannett different from the troubled *New York Times* and newspapers in other metropolitan areas? How much would our earnings improve this quarter, this year, next year?"[7] Gannett delivered the goods: It would report increasing profits, quarter after quarter, for twenty-two years, an incredible streak that would not be broken until the 1990 recession.

Many journalists were troubled by the new emphasis on stock values. "There was a time when *The New York Times* made the money in order to strengthen the news operation," says Bill Kovach, curator of the Nieman Foundation at Harvard University and a former Washington bureau chief of the *Times*. "The profit margin was 5, 6, 7 percent, and the Sulzberger family was perfectly content with that. The minute *The New York Times* had to go out to the market to raise capital, they had to play the Al Neuharth game. The market recognizes only one thing, and that's quarterly profits. That's the thing Al Neuharth brought to the newspaper business."

Automation broke the unions' stranglehold on newspaper production. Newspaper executives discovered that there was a whole

universe of readers out there who weren't vitally interested in government and diplomacy, and editors were finally figuring out ways of
reaching them. Hundreds of papers ginned up some imitation of the
Washington Post's irreverent "Style" section, which Benjamin Bradlee
launched in 1969, a savvy successor to the dowdy women's section of
fashion, weddings, and recipes.

In the Roaring Eighties, some newspaper stocks tripled in value as
Wall Street woke up to the companies' cash-cow potential. The New
York Times Company, which in 1975 had earned less than $13 million,
turned a profit of $266 million in 1989. The Washington Post
Company, which in 1975 had earned $12 million, made $197 million
in 1989. Other highly profitable newspaper companies that year
included Gannett ($397 million), Knight-Ridder ($247 million), Dow
Jones ($317 million), and Times Mirror ($298 million).

The media business was swept up in the takeover frenzy that saw
bigger and bigger corporations devoured by raiders and rivals.
Gannett bought the *Des Moines Register* and three smaller papers for
$200 million and the *Louisville Courier-Journal* for $306 million. The
Chicago Sun-Times was sold to a group of its executives for $145 mil-
lion, the Dallas *Times Herald* to William Dean Singleton for $110 mil-
lion, the Baltimore *Sun* and a television station to Times Mirror for
$600 million, the *Detroit News* and a television station to Gannett for
$717 million. Some papers, such as Ralph Ingersoll's short-lived *St.
Louis Sun* and Jack Kent Cooke's Los Angeles *Daily News*, relied on
junk bonds floated by Drexel Burnham Lambert. The stock of publicly
traded newspaper companies jumped 587 percent during the 1980s,
nearly twice the increase in the Dow Jones industrial average, according to an analysis prepared by John Morton of the brokerage firm
Lynch, Jones, and Ryan.

The family-run businesses were dying out, and chains were taking
their place. In 1930, there were fifty-five newspaper groups. In 1960, 109
newspaper groups controlled 46.1 percent of daily circulation, about the
same proportion as in 1930. By 1978, however, 167 groups controlled
72.2 percent of circulation, a dramatic increase. Those figures mask an
even greater concentration at the top. In 1978, the top five chains—
Gannett, Knight-Ridder, Hearst, Scripps-Howard, and Newhouse—already
controlled 23.2 percent of daily newspaper sales. By 1982, chains
accounted for more than 78 percent of total daily circulation.[8]

Some chains cut staff, slashed the news hole, and raised advertising rates. Ben Bagdikian has estimated that a corporation buying a
monopoly newspaper can use such methods to boost its profit margin
from 15 percent to 40 percent.[9] Editors are acutely aware of this. In one

survey, 62 percent of the editors at chain newspapers said their companies' concern for profits came at the expense of community interests.[10]

As chain ownership expanded and more and more newspapers died, head-to-head competition became increasingly rare. In 1923, 502 American cities had at least two daily newspapers. By 1953 that figure had dropped to 91, by 1963 it was 51, and by 1978 it was 35. In 1993, fewer than twenty cities had fully competitive newspapers. As major papers folded in Washington, Philadelphia, Los Angeles, Miami, Baltimore, Cleveland, Buffalo, Dallas, Anchorage, Pittsburgh, San Antonio, and elsewhere, 98 percent of American cities became monopoly towns, served by a single newspaper (or two papers owned by the same corporation).

Sadly, history has shown that each time a newspaper folds, many of its readers simply disappear. When the *Miami News* shut down in 1988, for example, the *Miami Herald* picked up only 15 percent of the 15,000 subscribers who were not already taking both papers.[11]

The veneer of competition has been preserved in twenty more cities—including Detroit, Nashville, Seattle, and San Francisco—through partial mergers known as joint operating agreements (JOAs). These government-blessed arrangements prop up failing papers by allowing them to share printing and business operations with a stronger rival. The idea, codified in a 1970 law pushed by the Nixon administration, is to preserve competing editorial voices, but the result has been to guarantee the partners hefty profits for decades, even if one paper shuts down. The concept appeared particularly perverted in 1986 when Al Neuharth of Gannett and James Batten, chairman of Knight-Ridder, arranged a shotgun marriage for the *Detroit News* and the *Detroit Free Press*, despite criticism that neither was truly a "failing" paper as required by law. Two years later, when Cox Newspapers shut down the *Miami News* under its JOA with the *Miami Herald*, it meant that Cox would receive a share of the *Herald's* profits until 2021.

This concentration of media power has taken its toll. The notion that a large conglomerate might have the same commitment to aggressive journalism as an owner who is part of the community is, for the most part, ludicrous. The kind of tough, grind-it-out investigative reporting that angers advertisers and risks libel suits is simply not high on the agenda of chain managers, or of chain editors, who often spend two or three years in a city before being promoted to a bigger market.

There are exceptions, of course. Knight-Ridder, during the 1970s and 1980s, improved many of the papers it bought, most notably the *Philadelphia Inquirer* (circulation 504,000), which relentlessly investigated municipal corruption under its crusading editor, Gene Roberts, a crusty Southerner and former *New York Times* reporter and editor who helped the paper win a closetful of Pulitzer Prizes. But even Roberts complained about corporate budget-cutting before stepping down in 1990 as Knight-Ridder entered an era of austerity.

To some corporate owners, a newspaper is less a journalistic venture than a bottom-line proposition, no different from a restaurant or a plastics factory. Family owners want to make money, too, but it is far easier for a distant owner who doesn't rub shoulders with readers and advertisers to pull the plug on a newspaper. When Houston publisher William Dean Singleton closed the Elizabeth, New Jersey, *Daily Journal* (circulation 36,000) in 1992, he said the city's ailing retail core would never recover and that he planned to invest his money in suburban papers. It is hard to imagine a local owner so casually writing off a 212-year-old paper and its community.

Sometimes newspapers are bought and resold like stocks and bonds. The Times Mirror Company bought the *Dallas Times Herald* in 1969, then sold it in 1986 to Singleton, who flipped it two years later to a longtime associate, John Buzzetta, and a group of investors. Buzzetta closed the 225,000-circulation paper in 1991, selling its assets to the *Dallas Morning News.*

Afternoon newspapers, once aimed at a blue-collar audience, have become particularly vulnerable. Afternoon circulation has dropped 42 percent since 1970. Afternoon papers in Richmond, San Diego, Louisville, Baton Rouge, Shreveport, Spokane, Durham, Charleston, Knoxville, Tulsa, and Portland, Maine, have folded or merged with morning editions in recent years.

The culture of the business changed during the 1980s as more companies grew accustomed to annual profits of 30 or 35 percent, twice as high as most American industries could ever hope to see. In a hundred different ways, some subtle, some blatant, many papers began to emphasize profits over journalism. "Jim Batten has to go to Wall Street several times each year and talk to analysts who are not really interested in the quality of Knight-Ridder newspapers," says Robert Haiman, president of the Poynter Institute for Media Studies and managing editor of the *St. Petersburg Times* from 1966 to 1976. "They tend to doze off and yawn when he talks about the incredible string of Pulitzer Prizes they have deservedly won, and they pop to attention in their chairs only when he begins to discuss next quarter's dividends. That is alarming."[12]

Luedtke says top newspaper executives have a vested interest in propping up stock prices, since many bought up large batches of the first stock issued by their companies. "It's awful hard for them to say, maybe we're not going to make 20 percent profit anymore, maybe it's going to be 15 percent," he says. "By taking these companies public, we created great numbers of millionaires out of the senior executives at the papers." Nor did the 1991–92 recession, which spurred so many cutbacks and so much belt-tightening, affect those in the executive suites of major newspaper companies, as Michael Skory, a contributing editor for *News Inc.*, has noted. Charles Brumback, president and chief executive officer of the Tribune Company, received $2 million in total compensation as the company's net income dropped 126 percent. Warren Phillips, chairman and chief executive officer of Dow Jones, received $1.8 million in total compensation as the company's net income dropped 66 percent.[13]

Newspapers were hit much harder by the 1991–92 recession than anyone had expected. Earnings plunged by 40, 50, even 70 percent at some companies. "The Party's Over," *Forbes* announced in a cover story. The classifieds, which had been the engine for spectacular growth, stalled with the collapse of real estate, automobile, and help-wanted ads. Department stores, the traditional linchpin of retail advertising, were in trouble. Some closed their doors, like Alexander's and B. Altman's in New York, and Garfinckel's in Washington. Others, like Macy's and Bloomingdale's, were bankrupted by debt-laden corporate takeovers.

Less advertising invariably meant less news. Most newspapers froze hiring and offered buyouts to induce older employees to quit. Others laid off staff, cut their news pages, and slashed travel budgets. Several papers, including the *Salt Lake Tribune* and the *Philadelphia Daily News*, closed their Washington bureaus. The *Wall Street Journal* sold its corporate jet, closed its Philadelphia bureau, and laid off several foreign correspondents. The *Philadelphia Inquirer* cut its news hole by as much as 12 percent and cut 130 jobs. The *Atlanta Journal-Constitution* laid off 133 employees and eliminated 122 vacant positions after failing to save enough money by turning off a third of their lights and making their own legal pads from recycled newsprint.

The *San Francisco Examiner* shrunk its news staff by 20 percent. The *New York Times* persuaded 160 employees to take early retirement and left another 25 editorial jobs vacant. The *Chicago Sun-Times* put its staff on a four-day work week. The New York *Daily News* declared bankruptcy. The owner of the *New York Post*, Peter Kalikow, declared bankruptcy. The Dallas *Times Herald* shut down. The *Anchorage Times* shut down. P. Anthony Ridder, president of

Miami-based Knight-Ridder, called 1991 "the worst year in the modern history of daily newspapers."[14]

Many papers responded by raising prices, and circulation took a nosedive. In the fall of 1991, sales dropped by 62,000 at the *Wall Street Journal,* 54,000 at the *Detroit News,* 38,000 at the *Detroit Free Press,* 35,000 at the *Milwaukee Journal-Sentinel,* 30,000 at the *Houston Chronicle,* 34,000 at the *Atlanta Journal-Constitution,* 32,000 at the *St. Louis Dispatch,* 21,000 at the *Houston Post,* 21,000 at the Baltimore *Sun,* and 19,000 at the *Los Angeles Times.* Newspapers were driving away the very readers they needed to survive.

Most of today's newspaper managers, Bill Kovach says, "came of age in the late '70s and the '80s, when they all thought they were geniuses. . . . Newspapers became one of the most profitable industries in the history of the country, second only to the oil industry. Suddenly things get bad and they start trying to maintain as much of that margin as they can, as if that was normal."

While virtually all publishers and editors insist they are not weakening their commitment to news, these declarations sometimes have a hollow ring. Thomas P. Geyer, publisher and chief executive officer of the *New Haven Register* (circulation 101,000), laid off 19 employees out of a staff of 740 in the fall of 1990 to cut costs. When he refused an order from the *Register*'s parent company to dismiss another 30 people, saying it would damage the paper, Geyer himself was sacked. A New York investment firm had bought the *Register* the year before for a reported $245 million, an extraordinary price for a small Connecticut paper, and was said to be under considerable pressure to meet its debt payments.

The sad truth is that most newspaper owners did little to prepare for the lean years. "They had a money machine," says John Morton. "They could put out a lousy-looking newspaper, not a very good editorial product, and they could get away with it because they were the only thing there was. Increasingly during the '80s, they were no longer the only thing there was. But you still find a lot of newspaper companies that emphasize the bottom line to the exclusion of everything else."

Reinventing the Newspaper: Four Attempts

As newspapers have tried to cope with the pressures of depressed profits, declining readership, and changing public tastes, they have taken very different paths. What follows are four case studies in how newspapers in different markets have tried to reinvent themselves, with very different results.

USA Today/McPaper

USA Today has become a shorthand phrase for all that is superficial about daily journalism: short snippets of news, glib writing, glossy packaging with little substance.[15]

From the moment of its 1982 debut, the Gannett paper did much to earn this reputation by honing its formula for low-calorie journalism. The newspaper establishment greeted *USA Today* with a rousing Bronx cheer: It was mediocre, junk food, McPaper.

But a funny thing happened on the way to the McPapering of America: *USA Today* got more serious. In the early 1990s it discovered hard news. Its stories grew a bit longer. It started providing reasonably good coverage of Washington, politics, the economy, health care, and other nuts-and-bolts issues. If General Motors announced it was cutting 74,000 jobs, that would be the lead story in *USA Today*, just as it was in the *New York Times*. It is, in my view, a much improved and more substantive newspaper, and while it still has shortcomings, its evolution toward more hard-edged journalism carries an important lesson for the industry.

Gannett executives realized that there was a financial reward in hard news. In 1991, the ten best-selling editions of *USA Today* were related to major news events. The paper sold an extra 1.3 million copies of a special edition at the outset of the Persian Gulf War. The day after basketball star Magic Johnson announced he had the AIDS virus, circulation jumped by 575,000. *USA Today* sold an extra 475,000 copies during the failed Soviet coup attempt.

"In the beginning we weren't sure if we could sell newspapers if we did the same stories everyone else did," says Peter S. Prichard, the paper's editor since 1989, who joined Gannett in 1972. "We tried real hard—probably too hard—to be different. If you look at our front pages the last couple of years, it's almost all hard news.

"We've discovered what journalists have always known, that hard news sells newspapers. But I don't think we've changed our emphasis on putting the reader first, on not being boring. Our philosophy is readers don't have much time and you've got to give them clear presentation and lots of entry points."

The renewed emphasis on news has won over some of *USA Today*'s earlier critics. "It's become a much more substantial newspaper just at the time all the apes are aping the thing that didn't work," Harvard's Kovach says. "This is the greatest announcement possible that readers want real news."

From the beginning, *USA Today* embodied a whole different approach to journalism. How the paper looked—its layout, its color photos, its eye-catching graphics, its little boxes filled with factoids—was as important as what it said. Articles were tight and bright, attuned to the lightning pace of the computer age. The paper was produced in Arlington, Virginia, and transmitted by satellite to thirty-two sites around the country where it was printed. The paper was sold from futuristic-looking boxes, and featured a paragraph of news from all fifty states and enough sports to satiate the most fanatic fan.

USA Today reflected the personality and outsized ego of Al Neuharth, a South Dakota maverick who joined Gannett in the early 1960s when it was a regional, sixteen-paper chain based in Rochester. He built Gannett into the nation's largest chain, with more than eighty newspapers and a skyscraper headquarters overlooking Washington. But Neuharth remained obsessed with the idea of creating "a national newspaper so informative and entertaining and enjoyable that it would grab millions of readers, including many of the television generation who were then nonreaders."[16]

In the first edition on September 15, 1982 (155,000 copies), there was a telling sign of what Neuharth called the "Journalism of Hope." A headline announced a plane crash with "Miracle: 327 Survive, 55 Die." In the following years, *USA Today*'s page-one stories included such fare as "Hitting Slots for Therapy," "Card Tells If You're under Stress," "Slopes Set for Record Ski Crowds," and "Enjoy Job, Live Longer; Other Tips."

"We were too unique," says Thomas Curley, *USA Today*'s president and publisher. "There were headlines like 'Men, Women: We're Still Different' and 'We Eat More Broccoli.' That ate at some of us, and it ate at our credibility."

That era has now passed. Tom McNamara, the managing editor for news, says the fascination with "silly and superficial crap" faded after Neuharth's 1989 retirement. "Those stories that used to be stripped across the top of the front page—'Women Have More Sex in Elevators'—they were the staples of morning disc jockeys, but they played to the belief that *USA Today* was not a serious newspaper," he says. Circulation has, nonetheless, continued to climb, from a daily average of 1.7 million in March 1989 to 1.9 million in March 1992.

The paper's culture evolved as veteran big-city reporters—including Patricia Edmonds from the *Detroit Free Press*, Adam Nagourney from the New York *Daily News*, and Tom Squitieri from the *Boston Herald*—joined a staff that Neuharth had largely assembled from small Gannett papers. "To be honest, three years ago we didn't have enough talent to compete . . . in the big leagues of journalism," McNamara said in a 1991 interview.

Staffers welcomed the new emphasis on news. Political writer Nagourney did a double take when he was asked to do a long piece on the economic positions of the Democratic presidential candidates. "The most boring story in America, but they pushed me to do that story," he says.

The front page, once filled with such headlines as "We Still Believe in American Dream," now featured stories on civil rights, hunger in Russia, and Middle East peace talks. The post-Neuharth paper tackled such complicated subjects as the health of life insurance companies. A page-one story about toxic dumping in minority communities—dubbed "environmental racism" by one critic—seemed less the "Journalism of Hope" than plain old journalism. Even Neuharth, who now writes a weekly column for *USA Today* and is the chairman of the Freedom Forum, a foundation focused on media, says the paper has "matured."

USA Today now blankets major news events, but slices the coverage into digestible chunks—seven pieces on the release of hostage Terry Anderson, eight on the William Kennedy Smith rape verdict. Gannett executives, realizing that news can be marketed, often boost the press on heavy news days. While the paper still hasn't turned a profit—indeed, it lost more than $800 million in the first nine years—it is second only to the *Wall Street Journal* in circulation. Once a second paper for people on the run, it is now the primary source of information for nearly 40 percent of its readers.

Gannett officials say the paper has been edging closer to profitability each year, although they suffered a setback in 1991 when the recession pushed *USA Today*'s losses to $18 million. Local newspapers, meanwhile, continue to borrow liberally from the *USA Today* formula because their economic base is very different. As a coast-to-coast paper with no hometown, *USA Today* must rely almost entirely on national advertising—cars, airlines, liquor companies, and so on—while the financial underpinning of any metropolitan paper is area department stores, grocery chains, and other retailers.

For all its improvements, *USA Today* has not quite sworn off the frothy stuff. On the day that Peter Prichard gave me a tour of headquarters, we came upon an artist preparing a computer graph on "Percentage of Adults Who Say They Sleep Nude." (For the record, it was 26 percent of men, 6 percent of women.)

The paper's limitations are obvious. It has no permanent foreign correspondents. Often the paper carries only one or two foreign stories a day, plus a column of briefs. There is little investigative reporting. Space in the news section is extremely tight. Some stories lack sophistication.

USA Today remains a paper that runs a banner headline when movie star Julia Roberts calls off her marriage to Kiefer Sutherland; that can offer seven front-page sentences on a coup in Haiti and pretend it is informing its readers; that panders to teenagers with a cover story on "Girls Who Go Gung-Ho after Guys/The Woo Is on the Other Foot for Boys Pursued by Aggressive Admirers"; that has the admirable goal of picturing a minority and a woman on each section front—but often fills the bill with the likes of Michael Jordan and Madonna; that puts out bonus sections like "Wheels" that are thinly disguised advertising vehicles, bursting with such upbeat stories as "Showrooms Loaded with Bumper Crop."

Still, even the most curmudgeonly critic would concede that *USA Today* changed the look of an entire industry. Once it appeared on the newsstands, other papers seemed hopelessly gray by comparison. By the late 1980s dozens of papers, from the *Boston Globe* to the *Chicago Tribune* to the *Miami Herald,* had switched to color presses. Editors started using more graphics as a way of quickly imparting information. A wave of redesigns, with fewer stories on the front page and more liberal use of white space, replaced the cluttered layouts of the past. Indexes and digests, offering brief summaries of the day's news, became standard equipment. Hundreds of sports sections expanded their coverage, adding lots of box scores and agate type. A big weather map became de rigueur.

Another innovation pioneered by *USA Today* is less visible to the reader. To compress reams of copy into bite-sized portions requires a top-heavy bureaucratic structure in which a single story is often rewritten by two or three editors. *USA Today* reporters sometimes work the phones for two days on a story that is boiled down to an eight-inch short. Key facts are lost in the process.

Philip E. Meyer, who teaches journalism at the University of North Carolina and who was director of news and circulation research for Knight-Ridder until 1981, says reportorial egos are invariably bruised at papers that have adopted this editor-intensive format, an approach that he thinks can be positive for newspapers.

"It changes the whole corporate culture of the newsroom because the reporter is no longer the star, it's the editor," he says. "Your words have to be pushed and pummeled and pounded to fit the format, which is not that much fun for writers."

A typical office joke: How many *USA Today* editors does it take to screw in a lightbulb? Ten—one to take it out, one to put it back in. One to take it out, one to put it back in. . . .

"Your story is never free from assault," says reporter Dennis Cauchon. "You may leave at 7 P.M. and think you're done, but it gets assaulted again by the night shift. They'll change your copy to reflect what's in the wire story, even though the wire reporter may be some twenty-three-year-old rookie.

"If you strip away the color, the graphics, it reads a lot like the AP," he says. "It's very standard. What's lost is style, personality, voice, and flavor. People aren't going to buy you because you're the local paper and they need the grocery ads. You really have to be more interesting."

One staffer doesn't think much of the Neuharth holdovers: "The place is still peopled with a lot of castoffs from mediocre newspapers. . . . Their editorial page should be nuked off the face of the earth."

At the same time, this staffer says, "They're getting away from the silliness and short stories and triteness of the early years. Their goal is to be a news magazine each day. They're willing to spend money like crazy to be taken seriously on a story."

The 25/43 Project

Knight-Ridder newspapers, including the *Philadelphia Inquirer*, *Miami Herald*, and *Detroit Free Press*, have always stood for quality. In recent years, however, the nation's second-largest chain has grown fixated on cultivating new readers, particularly the baby boomers so prized by advertisers. The new Knight-Ridder era is marked by constant talk of readers as "customers." "Too many editors and reporters think there's something demeaning and unworthy—'pandering' is the favorite epithet—about making newspapers entertaining and enjoyable," says James K. Batten, the company's chairman and chief executive officer. "I think that's nonsense."

Batten's answer to Gannett's *USA Today* is the 25/43 Project, a $2 million effort aimed at designing a newspaper that appeals to affluent readers in that all-important age group.

For years, the *Delray Beach News* was an aging, black-and-white dowager, not terribly different in tone and content from hundreds of other small-town papers. But in 1989 the Knight-Ridder paper's name was changed to the Boca Raton *News* and in the fall of 1990, the *News* was reborn as a pastel-colored hodgepodge of snippets of news. It is sold from pink newspaper boxes, and its logo is emblazoned with a pink flamingo standing on one leg.

There was a "Critter Watch," a daily data box about creatures from the Portuguese man-of-war to the gopher tortoise. There was "Today's Hero," an upbeat little blurb meant to "tell a good story about someone each day." There was "Success" offering "close-up looks at the careers of area professionals who are striving and succeeding . . . topics of style and manners that help you shine on the job." There was an absolute rule: No story in the daily could jump from one page to another. And there were maps: One map for world news, another for national news, with little numbers keyed to the two- and three-paragraph briefs that passed for news stories. Yet another map was stripped across the top of the local news section, with crime and traffic shorts. It was called "News near You." Some of these features, such as "Critter Watch," have since been dropped.

A typical front page has three stories, a brief column by a local resident, and a large, pink-edged guide to other features called "30 Seconds," which is about how long it takes to read any story in the paper.

"A lot of what we do here I would not be proud of if I was still at the *Miami Herald*," says Lou Heldman, the Knight-Ridder executive who supervised the launch of the 25/43 Project and who was deputy managing editor at the *Herald* before that. "It's a different level of journalism. It does a good job of explaining the world for people who don't want the world in great depth."

Editors bragged about stories on children's temper tantrums or working women too busy to sleep. A thirty-five-paragraph *New York Times* story on "chronic anger" was sliced to five paragraphs and featured on page one. When the town's new movie complex raised its price from $6 to $6.50, that was also a front-page story, four inches long.

During my visit, Wayne Ezell, editor of the *News*, thumbed through a copy of that morning's *Miami Herald*. It was playing up a scandal involving the misuse of mortgage money. Pretty dull, he said. Then he turned to his own paper. "'Champagne Prices Soon to Explode'—we're the only paper in America to do an eight-inch story on that," he said. "For baby boomers who go to a lot of champagne parties, that's more interesting than whatever Jack Kemp had to say today."

Ezell boasted of changes that would make other editors cringe. "We're doing a lot less government stuff . . . and more this-affects-you features," he said. He spoke of the more than thirty focus groups during the start-up and the strategy sessions that decided on emphasizing short stories.

"Nobody with a reporter's mentality was allowed in these meetings," Ezell said. "Someone said, 'Maybe we shouldn't have any jumps.' There was a long pause. Reporters would have said, 'That's just crazy!'"

What was most striking about this journalistic melange is that Ezell and Heldman never talked about reporting. It was all cute columns and friendly features and Macintosh graphics. Very little of Knight-Ridder's

25/43 budget was spent on beefing up the staff of young reporters, none of whom made more than $25,000 a year. Most of the money went for more research, editors, graphic artists, and clerks.

I asked Ezell if he would stop carrying foreign news if focus groups pronounced it boring. "That would tell me they're not reading it, so why should I have it?" he said. "If readers said they wanted more comics and less foreign news, in a market-driven economy, I'm going to give them more comics and less foreign news."

The editors boasted of a jump in paid circulation, from 21,600 to 25,000, after the redesign, although the paper was being heavily promoted during that period and there were seasonal adjustments. But by the following year, circulation was up just 6 percent, to 23,628. Two circulation managers were fired for allegedly padding sales figures by including papers given away at shopping centers and special functions.

Many critics were not kind to the Boca Raton venture. "When *USA Today* first began publishing," Linda Ellerbee, president of a television production company, wrote, "I described it as a newspaper for people who find television too complex. In some ways, the Boca Raton *News* may be described as a newspaper for people who find *USA Today* too complex."[17]

"The more entertainment, the more celebrity, the more light news, the more graphics, the more color and pizazz that's stuffed into news-papers, the more irrelevant the newspaper becomes to the reader. . . . You become a memo, a tip sheet," Bill Kovach of Harvard says.

The *News* did come up with a few smart gimmicks. There is a daily guide to all the ads in the paper, as well as a guide on how to read the stock tables. The "Your Money" section, heavy on personal finance, is aimed at women readers—and a similar page now appears in the *New York Times.*

But the paper's tone is so boosterish it makes *USA Today* look dour. The opening of a new mall, Mizner Park, was greeted with a front-page column about the "tempting little designer shops" that ended: "Let's wish Mizner Park well." (Mizner Park placed advertisements in the paper.) There are special sections pro-duced by the advertising department, with such swooning cover stories as "Brown's Furniture and Design Has Never Looked Better" and "Al Hendrickson's Toyota Wraps Up a Record-Setting Year." The real estate section is filled with similar tales: "The Lakes at Boca Raton Offering Close-out Savings," one said; "Camino Realty Celebrates Two Decades of Personable and Professional Service," said another.

"I see the newspaper as an agent of prosperity in the community—not just an observer, but an active participant," said Stephanie Murphy, a real estate editor who later left to become a marketing consultant and freelance writer. "We're a business. As newspapers change, there is a much closer interaction between ads and news than [there] used to be. . . . I prefer to tell the good story, the happy story. I don't go looking for termites—that's not my role."[18] Murphy sounded as if she were working for the Chamber of Commerce, not a daily newspaper.

The news in Boca Raton is sometimes an afterthought to all that supershopping. On December 13, 1990, for example, the lead story, about President Bush's approval of food aid to the Soviet Union, weighed in at seven paragraphs. The resignation of Education Secretary Lauro Cavazos got five paragraphs. Proposed cutbacks in minority scholarships at Florida Atlantic University got a whopping eight paragraphs. This was news you could swallow with a single gulp.

During my visit, several reporters told me they were not happy with the new format. Each week, in addition to covering their regular beats, they had to turn out one profile, one "Today's Hero," and other vignettes.

"I get very, very frustrated having to cover a city council meeting in 18 lines," said Anne Marie Reidy, then the local government reporter. "You can't give very much context or very many quotes. If I get in one quote from each side, that's really miraculous, even if forty people are standing up and screaming."

"When people say to me 'where's the news?' they're looking for the depth and analysis that television doesn't give," Reidy added. "We're a little too close to television writing for my taste right now."

Reader reaction was mixed. One reader called the new format "a jumbled mish-mash" and an "abomination." Another said she liked "all the little extras" and "little conversation starters."

Steven Abrams, a member of the local city council, said the paper was covering "yuppie issues" instead of "the bread-and-butter government issues. I'd like to see more coverage of government." But his wife, Debbie, who is busy with their young child, said she liked the redesign: "I can find exactly what I'm interested in. It's a quick read, yet you feel you have some information."

Wayne Ezell was undeterred by the outside criticism. "Newspapers have failed to treat readers as customers and tailor the product to the interests of those customers," he said. "We are producing newspapers the same way we did twenty and thirty years ago, and our readers have run off and left us."

The impact of the 25/43 Project is being felt far beyond Boca Raton. Knight-Ridder officials have urged their other papers to learn from the Boca Raton experience in changing both their look and their content. In a similar vein, Gannett executives have tried to spread the *USA Today* gospel to their other properties, sometimes with unhappy results.

Trouble in Little Rock

The *Arkansas Gazette*, a gray, respectable paper that consciously modeled itself on the *New York Times*, was sold to Gannett in 1986. The company spent tens of millions of dollars transforming the *Gazette* into a full-color paper, peppered with page-one stories about zoo animals, cheerleaders, and children in need of organ transplants. Five years later, it was dead.

It would be unfair to blame the demise of the 167-year-old paper solely on the editorial makeover. The *Gazette*, which near the end had a weekday circulation of 164,000, was locked in a long and costly war of attrition with the *Arkansas Democrat*, which had almost closed the gap with sales of 142,000. Few analysts believed that the Little Rock market could support two newspapers indefinitely. But there is little question that the *Gazette*'s transformation from a staid, old-fashioned newspaper to a colorful and jazzy one was so dramatic that it alienated many longtime readers.

In short, the battle between the *Gazette* and the *Democrat* is a classic example of two newspapers competing for the hearts and minds of local readers, one owned by a local businessman and the other by a national chain. The *Gazette*'s fate also demonstrates how a shift away from hard news can be fatal.

Walter E. Hussman, Jr., whose grandfather founded the media company that now owns several newspapers and cable television stations, bought the afternoon *Arkansas Democrat* in 1974. The scrappy *Democrat* had just half the circulation of the stately *Gazette*, the oldest newspaper west of the Mississippi. By 1977, the *Democrat* was taking in just 19 percent of local ad revenue. Hussman asked Hugh Patterson, the *Gazette*'s owner, for a joint operating agreement, with the *Gazette* receiving 90 percent of the profits. But Patterson, who owned the more lucrative morning market, turned him down.

Stung by this rejection, Hussman declared war. In 1979, he switched to morning publication. He started giving away free classified ads. He lured the state's biggest department store, Dillard's, by offering it unlimited ads for $500,000 a year. He published fatter papers than the *Gazette*, and his circulation began to grow. But he lost millions of dollars a year, losses that had to be subsidized by his string of small-town papers.

"I didn't know diddly about a competitive market and I learned the hard way," Hussman says. But he wasn't about to give up: "I kind of like Little Rock. I've got a nice house here. All these advertisers are friends of mine. I didn't want to leave."

Hussman hired John Robert Starr, a native Arkansan and the long-time Associated Press bureau chief in Little Rock, as managing editor of the *Democrat*. Starr posed for the cover of *Arkansas Times* magazine in a helmet and army vest with a knife between his teeth, squatting on a *Gazette* newspaper box. Hussman considered firing him for the stunt, but it served notice that a street fighter had taken charge.

In 1984, it was Patterson's turn to sue for peace. He took the *Democrat* to federal court, charging that Hussman was trying to drive him out of business through predatory price cutting. Starr called his rivals "cry babies." Patterson lost the suit in 1986, and seven months later he sold the paper to Gannett for $51 million.

Gannett may not have realized it, but the *Gazette* had a rich legacy as the state's social conscience. Founded in a malarial swampland in 1819 when Arkansas was still a territory, the paper had been edited by the legendary J. N. Heiskell from 1902 until his death in 1972, when his son-in-law Hugh Patterson became the paper's editor. Heiskell believed that news sold newspapers and that it was his responsibility to keep a watchful eye on government. Two Pulitzer Prize trophies in the high-ceilinged lobby testified to the editor's courage in 1957, when the *Gazette* strongly supported the integration of Central High School, which until then had been all white. Advertisers boycotted the liberal paper, backed by the segregationist governor, Orval Faubus, and circulation dropped, but Heiskell stood firm.

By the time Gannett bought the paper, the *Gazette* was still top dog in the market. It had higher advertising revenues and sold more papers than the *Democrat*. Its carpeted newsroom, filled with rows of personal computer terminals, hummed quietly like an insurance company. Its staff was more seasoned and better paid than that of the *Democrat*.

Four blocks away, the *Democrat* was assembled in a dingy former YMCA building, with cramped desks and mismatched chairs arranged around file cabinets stacked so high you needed a ladder to retrieve the yellowed clips they contained. The few ancient computer terminals had to be shared by the staff.

Al Neuharth's media conglomerate quickly moved to give the dowdy *Gazette* a facelift. In 1987, the company asked Michael Gartner, a Washington-based consultant for Gannett who would later become president of NBC News, to evaluate its new acquisition. Carrick Patterson, who had stayed on as editor of the Little Rock paper, didn't think much of Gartner's suggestions. A war of memos ensued over the following months.

Gartner said the weather map was full of "useless tables" showing "water levels of seven rivers at thirty-seven different locations."

Patterson replied: "The river bulletin is very important in this agricultural and flood-prone state. . . . Are you just trying to make us mad with outrageous statements like this?"

Gartner: "The paper has no zip, no sparkle, no twinkle. . . . It is full of news you can't use. . . . You just don't get a feel for Little Rock by reading the *Gazette*."

Patterson: "Our readers, since they live here, already have a 'feel' for the place. If the Little Rock Planning Commission is going to rezone the vacant lot across the street from me I damn well want to know about it and expect my newspaper to tell me. I'm a lot more interested in that than in the fact that 37 percent of Arkansans like disco music."

Gartner: "The editorial page is quite unappetizing . . . editorials are incredibly long . . . invariably deal with leaden issues of little interest or importance to most readers."

Patterson: "We don't try to be dull, but neither are we Pollyannas who try to make the editorial page the functional equivalent of television 'happy talk.'. . . It is our duty to deal with issues that may not be obviously important or interesting but that have significant impact on readers' lives."[19]

Carrick Patterson recently recalled what he described as "pressure to conform. We'd go to these meetings in Washington and we'd be preached to about *USA Today* and how wonderful it was."

There were other intrusions. Gannett talked the editor into starting a "Business Monday," despite his protests that not much happened in Little Rock business on weekends. The section drew little advertising. Several feature sections were added, but early deadlines were imposed so they could be printed in color, and that made them seem flat and lifeless.

"They had utterly no understanding of news," Patterson says. "Good reporting to them was short stories and not covering meetings. You don't cover the city board of directors meetings because that's boring; you cover some kid who needs a new liver."

When the publisher, William T. Malone, ordered him to write an editorial in 1987 saying that newspapers should be exempt from the state sales tax, Patterson threatened to resign. A compromise was reached, but relations remained strained. The paper was floundering. It became clear to Patterson that Gannett didn't know what it was doing.

"This is the thing that really gets to me: There did not seem to be a plan," Patterson says. "I certainly couldn't believe that this multi-billion-dollar company that had eighty straight quarters with increased revenues wouldn't be smart enough to manage the business. The direction for this month was, 'Let's spend a bunch of money and drive the bastards back.' The direction the next month was, 'Oh my God, we're spending too much money.' The staff was becoming more and more depressed."

Patterson was eased out as editor that fall and replaced by Walker Lundy, a veteran of newspapers in Fort Worth, Tallahassee, Charlotte, and Detroit. To much of his staff, Lundy seemed obsessed with human interest stories and color pictures. He ran front-page stories about the circus coming to town, new gorillas at the zoo, sick children, a baby born in the back seat of a car. One classic headline said, "Arkansans Encounter Visitor from Outer Space" (for a story about a meteor sighting). Some headlines carried exclamation points. Much national and foreign news was reduced to one- or two-sentence digests.

"The *Gazette* was like an elegant old woman and suddenly she was made to look ridiculous," said Alan Leveritt, now copublisher of the *Arkansas Times* weekly newspaper. "We had cheerleaders wearing spandex suits on the front page. That was just a little radical for us."

But Lundy viewed himself as an innovator trying to rescue a newspaper that had been declining for a decade. If the staff made fun of his fondness for "hero stories," well, that just showed they didn't understand what the average person liked to read. When anyone invoked the old chestnut about the *Gazette* being the *New York Times* of Arkansas, Lundy would remind them that the *Times* was not even the best-selling paper in New York.

"My belief is that up here are the readers," Lundy says, holding his hand at eye level. "Their lives are changing, their interests are changing. You drop about a foot down"—now he's at chest level—"and here come newspapers; we're changing too, but we're behind the people. Then you drop down another foot and there you find a lot of reporters, who believe newspapers are pandering to readers—God forbid you should do that— and trying to suck up to readers. They think you should keep doing what you were always doing, and fuck the readers. Most of them are too stupid anyway to be on a newspaper subscription list."

Still, Lundy was surprised at how local folks resisted his efforts to brighten the paper. "Arkansas really is a different state," he says. "In some respects the atmosphere there is the 1950s." He recalls one well-educated Little Rock woman who hated the fact that the *Gazette* had switched to color, though she couldn't quite explain why. "It was as if she was saying that God meant newspapers to be in black and white," he says.

Lundy tried to answer his critics in a 1988 column: "What's happened to the *Arkansas Gazette*? Well, here's the answer. We've gone after more readers."

The problem was the new *Gazette* was alienating many of its old readers. Although it was outspending the *Democrat* by $10 million a year, the *Gazette*'s circulation began to slip in September 1989 while the *Democrat*'s kept climbing. But both papers were awash in red ink.

Gannett also suffered a setback in spring of 1988 when William Dillard, chairman of the department-store chain and an old friend of Hussman's grandfather, got angry about a negative story about his company. Dillard promptly pulled his daily full-page ads from the *Gazette*. This cost the paper $2 million a year, but that wasn't the worst of it. Dillard's was the only full-service department store in town; now readers couldn't find out if Dillard's was having a sale by reading the *Gazette*. Other advertisers soon followed Dillard's lead.

Walker Lundy was dumped in 1990 and replaced by Keith Moyer, a Gannett editor from the Fort Myers, Florida, *News-Press*. A new publisher was imported. The *Democrat* ridiculed the revolving cast of managers as out-of-state "Gannettoids." Hussman appeared in television commercials, stressing his local roots as proprietor of "Arkansas' Newspaper." The *Democrat* even used the state flag as part of its logo. And a vitriolic column by John Robert Starr gave the *Democrat* a vivid working-class identity.

"The one thing they had going for them is that they were aggressive," Moyer says. "They were kick-you-in-the-nuts feisty. We always felt we were operating with one hand tied behind our back because we were the big corporation. We played by the rules, and they would come from behind and trip us up. The thought that Gannett was bad, the constant drumbeat in Starr's column, eventually caught hold with a certain segment of people in the state."

Hussman dismisses the charges of Gannett-bashing. "I don't think Gannett is an evil company," he says, but adds: "For a company that prides itself on research—the new buzzword—I don't think they understood the feeling readers had toward that paper. They really did turn it into a version of *USA Today*. They took the attitude that we know more about the newspaper business than anyone in America.

"The fact is, our editors were more attuned to what people wanted. Bob Starr grew up in Arkansas. I know a lot about Arkansas. Every week I make lots of story suggestions. I clip things out of the paper when we screw something up. You can't beat that kind of personal attention."

Keith Moyer toned down the *Gazette*'s emphasis on airy features. "Clearly, some of the moves that were made were wrong," he says. "We went back to being a serious newspaper and got away from some of the frivolous things Walker introduced."

Well, almost. Moyer still ran such front-page stories as "Porky the Warthog Found Dead at Zoo" and "Miss Arkansas Follows in Mother's Footsteps." He devoted a full page to brief items from far-flung counties that mimicked *USA Today*'s fifty-state digest.

As part of Gannett's "News 2000" program, an effort to put its newspapers in touch with the needs of their communities, Moyer ran a survey asking readers what they liked. It was paint-by-numbers journalism: Readers could check off whether they wanted more news from Europe or the Middle East. News about the governor. News about the legislature. News from your county. News from other Arkansas counties. News from Little Rock. Or from Column B: Coping with infants and preschoolers. Advice on teenagers. Advice on dating, sex, relationships. Advice on retirement. Single parenting.

One advantage of the competition was that Little Rock got far more news than most cities its size. But much of it was devoted to trivialities. There were constant attempts to scoop the other guy, or to knock down his story if he scooped you first.

"We run twelve-page sections on second-rate floods. . . . If they're going to emphasize fluff, we're going to have more and better fluff," Starr said in a 1991 interview.

In the final analysis, the *Democrat* was a mediocre newspaper. The *Gazette* had better Washington coverage. Its investigative reporting had brought down the state attorney general in 1990. Its political coverage was more balanced than that of the conservative *Democrat.*

The *Gazette*'s staff was 16 percent black, including several black managers and a black columnist; the *Democrat* newsroom was virtually all white. The *Democrat* had an embarrassing rule that no columnist could criticize Hussman's advertisers. Some readers grew tired of Starr's rantings, comparing the *Democrat* to the *National Enquirer.*

"The *Democrat* could do lousy reporting and people would say, 'Well, that's just the *Democrat*,'" Moyer says. "But the *Gazette* was the grand old paper. The *Gazette* was held to a higher standard."

Gannett officials were puzzled; the formula had worked for them at dozens of other papers. But they had forgotten that each city has its own tastes, its own idiosyncrasies.

For all its flaws, Walter Hussman's newspaper had its finger on the state's pulse. While slightly trailing in weekday circulation, it passed the *Gazette* on Sundays, 236,000 to 222,000. Hussman was still losing about $10 million a year, but he seemed willing to sustain those losses indefinitely. Gannett, however, was losing a staggering $25 million a year. That was intolerable for a publicly owned company.

"I'm not sure that newspaper was salvageable in any form," says Lundy, now editor of the St. Paul *Pioneer Press Dispatch*. "The truth is, if you're paying seventy-five cents for hamburgers and selling them for a buck, and the guy down the street is selling them for fifty cents, and he's willing to sell those seventy-five-cent hamburgers for fifty cents until he's old and retired, there's really not any way you're going to make money. When you strip away all the baloney—Was the newspaper soft? Was it hard? Was it fluffy?—there's no way you can compete in that marketplace. Gannett thought Hussman was willing to play by the normal rules of capitalism, and he wasn't."

In the spring of 1991, Gannett threw in the towel. Company officials, who did not want their capitulation to become public, secretly offered to sell Hussman the *Gazette*'s assets. When Hussman saw the books, he was stunned: Gannett had outspent him by $50 million over five years.

Rumors were rampant, but Gannett officials remained silent as they searched for a buyer. Everyone knew the end was near, but Gannett refused to say a word or allow the planning of a final edition. A *Democrat* photographer was attacked and received thirteen stitches after taking pictures of *Gazette* staffers leaving with their possessions.

On October 18, 1991, Gannett announced that it was closing the *Arkansas Gazette* that day and selling the assets to Hussman for $68.5 million. Seven hundred people were out of work. Company officials refused to discuss the matter; Gannett put out a terse statement saying the decision had been "influenced by market research conducted in 1990 that showed marginal prospects for increases in circulation penetration, despite reader satisfaction with the efforts to improve the *Gazette*." But no amount of corporate blather could mask Gannett's failure. The company had never figured out how to run an Arkansas newspaper from its Arlington, Virginia, headquarters.

John Brummett, who was the *Gazette*'s top political editor and columnist and who now writes for Hussman's paper, the *Democrat-Gazette*, says that Gannett "changed the soul of the paper. An old gray lady, a southern imitation of the *New York Times*, was transformed into pop journalism."

Walter Hussman put it this way:

> Having a newspaper here in Little Rock meant a lot more to me than it did to the people at Gannett. We live here. We worked harder. We realized we didn't have as much money and we had to be smarter.
>
> A Gannett paper might make a 35 percent pretax profit. Just think what you could do if you settled for 30 percent and added the other 5 percent to the newsroom budget. I want to put out a great newspaper. If this newspaper was located a thousand miles from here, I'd be less concerned about it. That's the advantage of local ownership. There's pride in the product.

The New *New York Times*

Twice in the past twenty years, the *New York Times* has been forced by financial pressures to expand its coverage and change the tone of the paper. The first makeover, when the *Times* went to four sections in the mid-1970s, is widely seen as having saved the newspaper. The jury is still out on the results of the more recent effort, a major overhaul in 1991 of the metropolitan section and the sports coverage. But what is most encouraging is that it is an investment in better journalism, and that company executives made the move with no expectation of an immediate increase in profits.

In a larger sense, the *Times*, which boasts a daily circulation of 1.1 million, is a textbook example of an old-fashioned newspaper dragging itself into the late twentieth century. There has been a "cultural revolution" at the paper, as Assistant Managing Editor for News John M. Lee put it, and the reverberations are still being felt.

For most of this century, the *Times* front page was a dependably dull repository of official pronouncements about matters of state. The front page of January 2, 1970, was crammed with eleven stories across eight narrow columns, nearly all of them official news: "Nixon

Promises an Urgent Fight to End Pollution"; "Administration Expects to Seek ABM Expansion"; "Agnew Ends Visit to Vietnam"; "Narcotic Arrests Up Sharply Here"; "Transit Strike Is Averted with 18% Wage Increase"; "Israel Rejects French Charges." The only color story, by Max Frankel, was "Mood in Capital: Change Will Be Slow."

Change was equally slow in the newspaper business. The two-section *Times* of that era shows how archaic the designs were. Half the front of the B section was devoted to an unsightly news summary. There was no clear beginning or end to local news or sports, since sections were not marked. The business and finance pages were jammed with fourteen stories, most involving corporate statistics. There was no op-ed page, no exploration of social issues, not a single graphic.

Faced with the prospect of major losses in the mid-1970s, A. M. Rosenthal, then the executive editor, and the paper's business executives decided to create some new sections. A Yankelovich survey confirmed Rosenthal's view that more people liked the *Times* than bought it regularly. The challenge was to draw them in without changing the basic character of the paper.

Rosenthal describes the strategy as "putting more tomatoes in the soup instead of more water. You can cut costs till your eyeballs bubble, or you can improve it, give yourself a better thing to sell."

The new additions—first "Weekend," followed by "Living," "Home," "Sports Monday," and "Science Times"—were dismissed by some as too frivolous for the *Times.* "My feeling was, if we were going to have food, it was going to be as good as the foreign report," the former executive editor says. "The asparagus stories would be as good as the stories from Paris." The new sections proved magnets for advertising—some, like "Science Times," did award-winning journalism as well—and helped carry the paper into the boom years of the 1980s.

A hallmark of the old *Times* was its heavy-handed copy desk, which labored mightily to impose the same constipated style on all writers. When Molly Ivins, the Texas columnist now at the *Fort Worth Star-Telegram,* worked as a reporter at the *Times* in the late 1970s, she described a man as having "a beer gut that belongs in the Smithsonian." The desk changed it to "a man with a protuberant abdomen." On another story, her description of a fellow who "squawked like a two-dollar fiddle" was recast as "an inexpensive musical instrument."

"I always felt like a horse shut up in a very small stall," says Ivins. "I kept kicking to get out. There was an enormous amount of institutional grayness built into that paper. . . . For a writer to work there is truly the death of a thousand cuts."

The new sections, such as "Living" and "Home," clearly helped to brighten the paper. They demanded better writing, since no one wanted to read a soporific story about asparagus. And that virus, once unleashed, gradually infected the rest of the paper. By the mid-1980s, Rosenthal and Managing Editor Arthur Gelb had brought in such talented writers such as Anna Quindlen, Maureen Dowd, Howell Raines, William Geist, Leslie Bennetts, and Joyce Maynard.

Complete *perestroika* for writers would not arrive until the Max Frankel era. The paper's persona lightened considerably after Frankel succeeded Rosenthal in 1986. Frankel understood that the business was changing, and not even the good gray *Times* could ignore the influence of *USA Today*.

The new front page, which usually has seven stories, more frequently dealt with such eclectic subjects as urban pigeons, yo-yos, rising hemlines, three-star French chefs, health-conscious dinner parties, rodeos, interracial marriages, the Mommy track, menopause, goose liver, teenage tennis camp, and the growing number of New York pizza parlors named Ray's (accompanied by a taste test).

One vivid page-one piece began: "You say you've had your European tour, your Caribbean cruise, your Club Med, your spa. You say you've bed-and-breakfasted New England, barged through Burgundy, hiked the Rockies. . . . Thousands of Americans are packing for a different kind of journey this summer. Destination: a higher spiritual plane."[20]

Says editorial page editor Howell Raines: "People say the front page is lighter now and we've lost gravitas. My feeling about the *Times* is we have so much gravitas that it doesn't hurt to lose a little. We've got to engage the reader in a different way. It's possible to be intellectually serious about something other than arms control and the Middle East and national infrastructure."

Joseph Lelyveld, the managing editor since 1990, describes the shift this way:

> We used to cover a lot of legislative process stories— "The House Ways and Means Committee voted yesterday 12 to 5 on the capital gains tax." It comes out of the Senate Finance Committee: front page. It comes out of the Senate: front page again. It goes to the joint committee: front page again. Signed by the president: front page again. The same thing on major legislation in Albany, Trenton, City Council of New York. We now look for the moment when the debate is sort of crystallized.

Long Island. While it could never cover every local sewer hearing like the *Record* in New Jersey or the *Hartford Courant* in Connecticut, it would concentrate on broader regional themes that might interest readers from Paterson to New Haven.

"We cover Manhattan well," Lelyveld says. "We cover city and state politics well. We never felt that what we were doing in the outer boroughs and the suburbs was up to the standards of the rest of our journalism."

Times executives had no expectation that beefing up the local staff would immediately improve the bottom line. It was, they say, more of a long-term investment. "Nobody has said this will increase our circulation by X and our revenues by X and if it doesn't do that it's a failure," said Assistant Managing Editor for Metro and Sports David R. Jones.

The number of suburban reporters was doubled. The city staff was beefed up in Brooklyn, Queens, and the Bronx. The Metro section got a glitzy new look, with *USA Today*-style graphics and an index with Boca Raton-type maps. "We are trying to address issues that have a universal theme," says Gerald M. Boyd, the metropolitan editor. "Everyone cares about transporation, taxes, property values. The challenge is to go beyond that, whether it is worrying about kids or the environment or the quality of schools, and find a way to present it so no matter where you live in the region, you're interested."

Bringing local news alive is not easy, and the Metro section still has plenty of dull stories on traffic and trash pickup and town libraries. Occasionally there is an in-depth look at a local newsmaker or trend, and now and then the writing sparkles, but the section has had trouble rising above the more pedestrian fare of daily crime and government budgets.

Still, the *Times* seems to be inching in the right direction. The paper even started a Sunday style section, and while many critics dismissed it as frivolous and sophomoric, the section labored mightily to be trendy with features about nightclubs, fashion, relationships, and gossip. "This is like changing the Soviet Union," Anna Quindlen says. "It doesn't happen overnight."

The State of Newspapers, Present and Future

As the case studies clearly indicate, newspaper editors are acutely aware of their readership problem. In response to research conducted for the *Washington Post*, here is what some occasional readers had to say about newspapers:

"It's something to do with my eyes while I'm eating lunch."—Male, 35–55

"When you see a plane crash, you are glued to that screen. With a newspaper, you can just throw it down."—Male, 18–34

"When you tell me about the Trident X sub missile, forget it. . . . I don't know who the heck they're aiming at. I don't know people that talk like that."—Female, 18–22

"I think headlines can keep you well informed. I don't like to start off the day on a negative note, and I think if you know too many of the details, it's negative. My job is depressing enough."—Male, 18–34

"The rapes and murders and stuff is what you're going to read. . . I don't relate to world news."—Female, 18–22

"I hate getting ink on my hands."—Male, 35–55

"I don't want people to see me as stupid. That's really the only reason I read."—Female, 18–22

"I can't take a newspaper every day. It's just too much of an information blitz coming at me."—Male, 18–22

While I don't think much of the way in which some editors use market research as a bible, such comments obviously illuminate the wide gap between newspapers and their readers, particularly younger readers. Nicholas Androulidakis, the consultant who did the interviews, says many young people have little interest in the world beyond their small circle of friends and colleagues. "They hear in their newspaper the voice of their parent, their teacher, some other authority figure," he says. "They don't hear their own voice, the voice of their friends."

The implications for the republic are not encouraging. A 1990 survey by the Times Mirror Center for the People and the Press, based on 4,890 interviews of people aged eighteen to twenty-nine, concluded that young Americans "know less and care less about news and public affairs than any other generation of Americans in the past fifty years." It is hardly surprising, therefore, that these young people have little use for newspapers.

Nearly every newspaper in America is working on the problem. The *Wall Street Journal*, with the nation's largest circulation, has started a classroom edition. The *Fresno Bee* (circulation 149,000) publishes a weekly "Teen Tempo" section. The *Washington Post* (838,000) started an "Under 21" page, but quickly scrapped it as substandard.

"If you treat kids as if they're somehow inferior and should be put off in a corner, they don't like it," says Robert G. Kaiser, the *Washington Post*'s managing editor. "They have a place in our world. I'd like our pop music coverage to be so good that if you're really into rock 'n roll, you're going to learn stuff that's going to make you look cool with your friends."

The *Syracuse Herald-Journal* (circulation 89,000) delivers its weekly youth tabloid, called "hj," to thirty-one area high schools each Thursday. "Newspapers traditionally have covered a school by going to a school board meeting and covering the budget," says youth editor Larry Richardson. He has hired a network of high school stringers who get $15 a story "to report things that the school PR departments don't tell us."

While some of the dispatches concern cars and beer parties, the school correspondents have also reported on sexist remarks by a vice principal and a controversial "Slave Day" held during Black History Month. Some principals "try to shame the students into not writing a story because it makes the school look bad," Richardson says.

The "hj" section covers such topics as status sneakers, cheerleading, radio, dieting, class cutups, weightlifting, smoking, drinking, and dating. A "What's Hot" column (nose earrings, untied shoes, spiked hair, ripped jeans) keeps kids apprised of fashion trends. In the Monday paper, brief profiles of a half-dozen students, known as "Class Acts," have proven popular with readers.

If all this sounds like a throwback to the days when newspapers ran pictures of newborn babies and senior citizens who bowled three hundred, it may be no accident. Steve Crosby, executive editor of the Lafayette, Indiana, *Journal & Courier* (circulation 38,000), says newspapers have started "taking us back twenty years to the time when we weren't too important to put in their engagement announcements, or when the community group is going to meet, and other things people want to read. We sort of lost that homey touch. I call it chicken-dinner news. Staffs hate it; readers love it."

A growing number of papers are concluding that the future is local, local, local. The *Hartford Courant* (circulation 229,600) has subdivided itself into seven zoned editions that cover eighty-two communities across Connecticut. Each edition contains different "Our Towns" editorials, different letters to the editor, and different photos, along with such items as school lunch menus and women's club activities. The bureaus are divided into "A" towns, where reporters must file a story every day, and smaller "B" towns, where the quota is at least a news brief every day. The sports staff has been expanded to cover the action at 118 high schools, all of which have parents who want to read about their kids' exploits.

"It's extremely expensive, but we believe it's our franchise," says Managing Editor David S. Barrett. "We've become known as the bible for scholastic sports in Connecticut." Not coincidentally, these zoned sections also appeal to small advertisers, who can reach a more limited area at lower rates.

The problem is that reporters assigned to such sections often feel like second-class citizens stranded in the boonies. The *Courant*'s local section is filled with such stories as "Town to Have New Tree-Cutting Policy" and "Woman Honored for Founding Orphanage." No journalists worth their word processors want to write about chicken-dinner news when they could be covering city hall scandals. And that makes it harder for editors to staff these zoned sections with experienced reporters.

The *Orange County Register,* one of the country's most innovative papers, has invented the ultimate suburban beat: the mall. "Some of these malls get fifty thousand to sixty thousand people a day," says reporter Jennifer Lowe, who won the paper's 1990 "Writer of the Year Award" for her efforts. "One mall here gets more people a year than Disneyland. We're trying to reach people in their everyday lives."

Lowe has written about mothers and daughters shopping together, people who hate malls, teenage shopping power, and a bathing suit chain where the clerks all wear swimsuits. Despite some colleagues' snickers, she has even written about the bathrooms at Orange County's eleven regional malls. "If you've ever gone shopping," Lowe says, "you need to find one."

The *Register* also runs daily reader polls on different questions, including inviting people to submit "life letters" about a loved one who recently died. "They're amazing," says editor Tonnie L. Katz. "They are very touching. They write about their neighbors, teachers, friends, cousins, fathers. They feel they have a stake in the paper. . . . We'll have seven hundred to fifteen hundred people a day calling us, faxing us. It blows my mind."

Such invitations are clearly an attempt to repair that frayed bond between readers and their newspapers. Readers have written to the Portland *Oregonian* about the oldest things in their refrigerator, to the *Deseret News* about their worst dates, to the *Dallas Morning News* about who killed Laura Palmer (a character in television's "Twin Peaks"), to the *St. Petersburg Times* about getting an abortion. They have entered a country song contest at the *Houston Chronicle,* offered Christmas fiction to the *Asbury Park Press,* and sent "sport coats from hell" to the Los Angeles *Daily News.*

In a more serious vein, the *Minneapolis Star Tribune* has assigned a reporter to cover family issues. The *Plattsburgh Press-Republican* (New York) has a reporter work a different job each week and write a first-person account of what it's like. The *Modesto Bee* (California) has led a get-out-the-vote drive. The *Portland Press-Herald* (Maine) has invited the public to its editorial-board meetings. The *Wooster Daily Record* (Ohio) has sponsored an annual book fair.

Even the biggest newspapers are working overtime to broaden their appeal. The *Chicago Tribune* has launched a weekly section called "Womannews," featuring such stories as women in the military, women who climb walls, self-defense for school girls, sexual chemistry, pregnant television anchors, PMS, infertility, yoga, and office gossip.

The *Wall Street Journal* is trying to boost its market share with businesslike precision. While planning to expand to three sections in 1988, says former executive editor Norman Pearlstine, "We went through twenty-two prototypes, which came to be known as 'putting lipstick on the pig.' "

The pig, of course, was nuts-and-bolts business coverage. But since many companies were laying off middle managers with company-paid subscriptions to the *Journal,* the editors had to look elsewhere for readers. They added legal coverage in an attempt to lure some of the nation's 750,000 lawyers. They added media and advertising coverage to establish a presence on Madison Avenue. When surveys found that most readers took up the *Journal* in college, the circulation department started pushing it on campus.

"A lot of our readers read us more out of fear than love," Pearlstine said before leaving the paper in 1992. "I'd like to see us become a wanna-read instead of a must-read." The new sections have improved the *Journal*'s readability, but circulation dropped sharply in 1991 after a price increase from 50 to 75 cents.

Since the late 1970s, the *Washington Post* has added sections called "Health," "Weekend," "Washington Business," and "Washington Home." A new "Style Plus" page has tackled such sensitive subjects as stress, bar hopping, romance, discussing sex with children, older women and younger men, divorce, alcoholism, retirement planning, and lesbian couples.

"Traditionally, American journalism was intimately tied to politics and government," managing editor Kaiser says. "I think we're trying to break that relationship, partly because politics has departed from real life. Flags and Willie Horton don't have much to do with real life. People are pissed off at that kind of symbol manipulation, and they're pissed off at us, too, for covering it.

"The assumption that the mayor, the city council, the chief of police, the congressman, and the president are among the most prominent newsmakers is a reflexive tradition. Lots of other people make news that's just as important to people's lives—real estate developers, sports figures, television personalities, owners of television networks."

In recent years the *Post* has added beats on race relations, lobbying, family issues, immigration, and high technology. The change is noticeable. In the fall of 1986, nearly all the *Post*'s front-page stories were of the hard-news variety—sanctions against South Africa, Senate races, local crime, Star Wars, plane crashes. In the fall of 1991, in addition to ordinary hard-news stories, there were page-one pieces on suburban traffic jams, innovative schools, students seeking help on their Scholastic Aptitude Tests, kids left motherless by crime, drivers who run red lights, food labeling, teenage boredom, middle-class renters who can't afford homes, and the frustrations of layoff victims.

Nearly all newspapers regularly indulge themselves with long series of articles. Far too many are interminable treatises on weighty issues—a lengthy *Newsday* series on trash comes to mind—that hold little appeal for ordinary citizens. Al Neuharth has a point when he says that many editors are obsessed with journalism prizes.

Ron Martin, editor of the *Atlanta Journal* (circulation 180,500) and *Atlanta Constitution* (circulation 316,000), says it is possible to combine in-depth reporting with the graphics-laden packaging of his previous employer, *USA Today*. Martin recalled a 1990 series by his Atlanta reporters on poverty and health care in the South. "It was wonderful, groundbreaking reporting," he says. But despite a splash that began with four full pages on Sunday, the series didn't get much reaction.

"We put together a number of focus groups," Martin says. "We said, 'Did anybody read this?' The bottom line was really no. There were one or two people out of two dozen who said they read the whole thing. That to me was a tragedy. I thought we as editors had failed them, that we had not figured out a way to tell them this was important, this was new.

"It's simplistic to say, are you doing 'Serious Journalism'? Are you doing investigative reporting? The question is, how are you doing it? How do you get into the heads of readers? Or are you making yourself feel warm all over because you've done your job, and the readers are just too dumb to get it?" Martin obviously believes the problem is not dumb readers but inadequate editing.

The central paradox of newspapers today is that they deliver more news more efficiently than ever before at a time when readers are drowning in information. Newspapers have many audiences, and it has become increasingly difficult to cater to one segment without driving away the rest.

The newspaper remains a mass medium, read by bureaucrats, housewives, teachers, cops, college students, and members of Congress, all with varied interests and obsessions. At the same time, newspapers cannot survive without making themselves indispensable to a sophisticated elite that demands detailed coverage of public-policy issues.

There is no magic formula, no all-purpose panacea for revitalizing newspapers. But we seem to have lost sight of the basics that once put the press at the center of our political and cultural life, as it was in the days of the civil rights struggle and the Vietnam War.

We must go back to the future, to a time when newspapers spoke the language of the streets and were not yet seen as arrogant and remote. At some point, says David Nyhan, whose *Boston Globe* column is syndicated nationally, "We stopped sweating for stories and settled for access. Sweating was reserved for workouts in sanitized health clubs, no smoking please. Spritzers replaced highballs. Our livers got healthier, our cardiovascular ratings soared. But where we got weaker was in the vicinity of the heart."[21]

While the new beats, from shopping malls to race relations, are a start, the rigid architecture of newspapers often fails to reflect much of the outside world. Too many of our beats are based on buildings (the statehouse, the courthouse, the White House) and issues (transportation, health care). Despite the recent changes, news that is sociological or simply unorthodox still slips through our net. It has often been observed that the press slept through one of the biggest domestic stories of the century—the great migration of blacks from the rural South to the industrial North—because no one called a press conference to announce it.

What if newspapers wrote about life with the same passion we bring to sports? Think of all the elements in a sports section: Money. Injuries. Strategy. Drug abuse. Trades. Competition. Strikes. Statistics. Winning and losing. Big-mouth writers calling the manager a bum. Where else in a newspaper do you find that kind of passion? No wonder fans devour the sports section long after they have watched the main event on television. Even the *New York Times* now takes sports very seriously.

What do sports reporters know that the rest of us don't? In the cable era, after all, a devoted fan can watch a half-dozen baseball games on a good night (not to mention all manner of athletics on ESPN, the CNN of the jock world). Why bother to read about it the next day? Perhaps it is because sportswriters are so much more opinionated, hailing the heroes and kicking the goats with reckless abandon. Perhaps it is that they have such freedom to second-guess and analyze whether the sacrifice bunt was a blunder or the starting pitcher should've been lifted earlier. Perhaps it is their ability to soak up color from the locker room, or to translate the most arcane strategy into the language of the casual fan. Winners and losers are never quite so clear in the real world, of course, but surely journalists have much to learn about bringing everyday drama alive.

The notion that newspapers must make themselves necessary and distinctive is, simply put, a matter of survival. The list of competitors, from CNN and MTV to magazines and newsletters to computer data services, grows longer every year. Many people are already convinced they can get all the information they need or want from television. As Frank Denton points out in his paper, that just isn't so.

It is my contention that newspapers, at their best, offer something different, more detailed and contextual than television, more immediate than magazines, more literary than newsletters. Only newspapers have the resources, the space, and the inclination to do serious investigative reporting and to hold public officials accountable for their actions. Only newspapers have the breadth to employ a staff that specializes not in one narrow area, but in subjects ranging from military affairs to medicine to the movies. Only newspapers can penetrate down to the neighborhood level while still serving up national news, sports, the arts, and so on. The detailed conversation of a presidential campaign, for example, is largely carried on in newspapers, while television offers viewers a shorter, punchier version each day. In short, newspapers help people make sense of the blur of images that swirl around them each day—and you can roll it up and take it on the bus.

But none of this matters very much if newspapers fumble away their basic franchise and are regarded by readers as disconnected from their daily lives. Here, then, is a sampling of what newspapers need to do more of:

▲   Make people mad. Write about outrages and injustice. Don't be afraid to get folks riled up; it is better to be controversial than ignored. A good newspaper should be like the feisty columnist that readers love to hate but would never dream of missing. When the president tells an obvious fib, let's call him out on strikes. When the mayor blows a big decision, why not holler: Throw the bum out! If a big corporation is giving some poor soul the shaft, let's blow the whistle. The New York tabloids, for all their bluster, have a healthy sense of crusading for the little guy, but most newspapers rarely deviate from their studied, above-the-fray posture.

▲   Tell us things the authorities do not want us to know. We have become so obsessed with the latest middle-class comforts that we have drifted from our original mission of afflicting the comfortable. There is no shortage of malfeasance and misfeasance in public life, and even small examples—the Pentagon's $640 toilet seats, or John Sununu's frequent flying—have symbolic value. Let's wean ourselves from our obsession with inside baseball and start questioning the rules of the game.

▲   Make us laugh. Newspapers take themselves much too seriously. Let's pay less attention to the public-policy nerds and explore the lighter side of the human condition. There is no reason to grant Dave Barry a monopoly in this area; surely we can find more comic relief amid the depressing headlines.

▲   Touch readers in their daily lives. Too much journalism, like government, exists on an abstract plane that has little meaning for most readers. Let's sink our teeth into subjects that people care about—schools, housing, crime, day care, traffic, hospitals—in ways that get their juices flowing. We need to spend less time at city hall and more time in the neighborhoods. The great popularity of traffic columns in some major papers—"Road Warrior" in the *Record*, "Dr. Gridlock" in the *Washington Post*—shows that there is a thriving market for pothole-level journalism. Unglamorous stories about appealing a property tax bill or evaluating local doctors may not win any Pulitzers, but they might win over some disaffected readers. And talented writers can work wonders with ordinary-sounding beats, such as health care or "family issues," if editors give them enough elbow room.

▲   Break the shackles of mindless objectivity. One reason the press was unable to sound the alarm on the savings and loan debacle is that we have become the prisoner of experts. Had more reporters trusted their instincts and made the case that the industry was collapsing, many billions of dollars might have been saved. Fairness and balance are essential, but hiding behind the old he said/she said formulas is a convenient copout. When the *Seattle Times* reported the charges of eight women who said they had been sexually harassed by Senator Brock Adams, it was, in effect, taking a stand against such conduct. The *Des Moines Register*'s powerful series on the rape of Nancy Ziegenmeyer fueled a national debate on how the courts and the media treat rape victims. If that amounts to activist journalism, so be it.

▲   Turn the writers loose. Serve up one magazine-quality piece each day that soars above the pedestrian. Let individual voices emerge from the bland chorus of daily journalism. We are a writer's medium; let's exploit that to the fullest. When newspaper columnists like Mike Barnicle or Mike Royko take aim at a juicy target, it is the talk of the town. The era when all news stories affected the same Olympian tone is over; we need to cultivate more writers who can peel the onion of multilayered subjects.

▲ Set the agenda. With few exceptions, the press remains a reactive instrument with an infant's attention span. We spend millions of dollars following the president around the globe and recording his every burp. We get wrapped up in campaign photo ops and attack ads. We swarm like bees into a department like Housing and Urban Development after the place has been looted, then buzz off in search of the next calamity. It is time to stop prospecting for official leaks and start digging up more news off the beaten path. In 1992, Charles E. Shepard of the *Washington Post* reported on the lavish spending habits of United Way of America's $463,000-a-year president William Aramony, including his chauffeured car service, Concorde flights, and expensive condominiums. The story not only led to Aramony's resignation but sparked a widespread reappraisal of how charities spend their money.

▲ Make it a picture medium. Newspapers must make better use of photographs to tell the story, particularly as we drag ourselves into the color era. Too many papers still publish too many pages of gray type. We need more arresting, more artistic photography that captures the moment, and fewer pictures of diplomats shaking hands. If the wordsmiths must sacrifice a few words to accommodate more pictures, so be it.

▲ Liberate the op-ed pages. The stuffed-shirt opinions proffered on these pages often range from A to B. While there are several provocative columnists around, we need to restrict the soporific lectures of people like Henry Kissinger and Jeane Kirkpatrick and throw open the gates to new, vibrant, even radical voices. The *Los Angeles Times*'s new "Voices" section, launched after the 1992 riots, is a step forward.

▲ Satisfy the specialists. Newspapers should offer regular features and columns for folks vitally interested in law, computers, publishing, science, religion, health care, personal finance, and so on. These should be accessible to the layperson but sophisticated enough to interest the aficionados. Such pieces won't appeal to everyone, but they help make the newspaper more like a modern supermarket and less like an old five-and-dime.

▲ Connect with the community. Anyone who's ever dialed a news-room and listened to the phone ring twenty times, or been bounced from one voice-mail recording to another, knows how remote the local paper can seem. We need to give people a sense that we're listening—by making it easier for readers to register complaints, get errors corrected, publish letters to the editor, track down old stories, or rectify subscription problems. More publishers should follow the example of the *Boston Globe, Washington Post, Chicago Tribune, Kansas City Star,* and thirty other papers that have hired an ombudsman to field complaints and criticize the paper internally. Editors should get out in the community—actually make it part of their job to do so—and every paper should have a senior editor who uses the opinion pages to explain its inner workings. We must lift the curtain of secrecy from the editorial process and do a better job of illuminating what we do.

The proliferation of special sections, from "Womannews" to "Teen Tempo," shows that we are reaching out to a fragmented audience. As the old, reflexive definitions of news begin to fade, many editors have been forced to think more creatively. But we must weave these threads into the fabric of daily journalism, rather than presenting them as occasional frills.

We know how to produce pastel-colored fluff like the Boca Raton *News.* We know how to produce serious newspapers like the *New York Times.* We know how to produce youth-oriented sections like the *Syracuse Herald-Journal.* But can we produce a single newspaper that will combine the strengths of all three? That will appeal to readers of the *Washington Post, Fortune,* and *Rolling Stone*? That, in a nutshell, is the challenge facing the industry.

The signs of change, even at tradition-encrusted places like the *Times,* are long overdue. But we are barely scratching the surface. Newspapers are still too homogeneous, too predictable, too weighted down by incremental news. What we need is fewer pink flamingos and more old-fashioned hell-raising.

Notes

1. Daily readership surveys were taken by the National Opinion Research Center, University of Chicago. Figures on teenage and adult readership of newspapers, juvenile books, and magazine circulation reported by David Shaw, "Young People Read, But Papers Aren't No. 1 Choice," *Los Angeles*

Times, March 16, 1989, pt. 1, p. 3. Also, Albert E. Gollin, "An Assessment of Trends in U.S. Newspaper Circulation and Readership," Newspaper Advertising Bureau, New York, December 1991.

2. Donald L. Barlett and James B. Steele, "How the Game Was Rigged against the Middle Class," *Philadelphia Inquirer,* October 20, 1991, p. A1.

3. Doug Underwood, "When MBAs Rule the Newsroom," *Columbia Journalism Review* 26, no. 6 (March–April 1988): 23.

4. Jean Gaddy Wilson, "For a New Nation, a New Press," *Nieman Reports* 46, no. 1 (Spring 1992): 17.

5. David Shaw, "Luring the Young: For Papers, Generation Is Missing," *Los Angeles Times,* March 15, 1989, pt. 1, pp. 1, 15.

6. The history of newspapers is drawn in part from Peter Stoler, *The War against the Press: Politics, Pressure, and Intimidation in the 80s* (New York: Dodd Mead, 1986); Michael Schudson, *Discovering the News: A Social History of American Newspapers* (New York: Basic Books, 1978); and Meyer Berger, *The Story of the New York Times* (New York: Simon & Schuster, 1951).

7. Allen Neuharth, *Confessions of an S.O.B.* (New York: Doubleday, 1989), p. 117.

8. Benjamin M. Compaine, *Who Owns the Media? Concentration of Ownership in the Mass Communications Industry* (White Plains, N.Y.: Knowledge Industry Publications, 1982), pp. 37–39.

9. Ben H. Bagdikian, *The Media Monopoly* (Boston: Beacon Press, 1990), p. 124.

10. Survey of editors at chain newspapers was reported in the 1990 Ownership Survey, American Society of Newspaper Editors, Reston, Virginia., April 1990.

11. Walt Potter, "Where Do Readers Go When Their Favorite Local Paper Dies?" *Presstime* 4, no. 4 (April 1992): 6.

12. Congressional Quarterly Editorial Research Reports, August 24, 1990.

13. Michael Skory, "Pay Dirt," *News Inc.* 4, no. 3 (March 1992): 23.

14. Tony Ridder was quoted by Thomas B. Rosenstiel, "1991 Has Been a Tough Year for the Media," *Los Angeles Times,* December 14, 1991, p. D2.

15. Valuable background information on *USA Today's* history was provided by Peter Prichard, *The Making of McPaper: The Inside Story of USA Today* (Kansas City: Andrews, McMeel & Parker, 1987).

16. Neuharth, *Confessions of an S.O.B.,* p. 107.

17. Linda Ellerbee, "Boca Watch/I Watched It on the Newspaper," *News Inc.* 3, no. 2 (February 1991): 21.

18. Elizabeth Lesly, "Realtors and Builders Demand Happy News . . . and Often Get It," *Washington Journalism Review,* November 1991, p. 20.

19. The Gartner-Patterson memos, Karl Cates, "Once-Great 'Gazette' Struggles to Find Identity in Gannett Era," *Arkansas Democrat,* April 28, 1991, p. 1.

20. Molly O'Neill, "A New Getaway: Bed, Breakfast, Spirituality," *New York Times,* July 17, 1991, p. 1.

21. David Nyhan, "Why They Don't Love Us Anymore," *Nieman Reports* 45, no. 4 (Winter 1991): 3.

Index

About the Authors

Frank Denton is editor of the *Wisconsin State Journal* in Madison. He has worked as an editor at the *Detroit Free Press* and as a reporter for newspapers in Texas, Alabama, and Ohio. He is a doctoral student in communications marketing at the University of Wisconsin-Madison.

Howard Kurtz is the *Washington Post*'s media reporter and author of the forthcoming book *Media Circus: The Trouble with America's Newspapers*. A veteran of the *Record* in New Jersey and the now-deceased *Washington Star*, his work has appeared in *Columbia Journalism Review*, the *New Republic*, the *Washington Monthly*, and *New York* magazine.